❧

## *Our Work, Our Words ...*

Hannah
I pray that our
words will help you
as you grow into the
young lady that this world
needs & truly tree change.
Thanks,
Nnamdi
Twin Poets

Enjoy our words
of truth & thank
you for listening to our
release & get yours a
journal & pen
& write
with it.

# Our Work, Our Words ...

## Taking the Guns from Our Sons' Hands

Twin Poets
Albert H. Mills &
Nnamdi O. Chukwuocha
Authors of Lyrical Libations

iUniverse, Inc.
New York  Bloomington  Shanghai

# Our Work, Our Words ...
## Taking the Guns from Our Sons' Hands

iUniverse books may be ordered through booksellers or by contacting:

iUniverse
1663 Liberty Drive
Bloomington, IN 47403
www.iuniverse.com
1-800-Authors (1-800-288-4677)

Because of the dynamic nature of the Internet, any Web addresses or links contained in this book may have changed since publication and may no longer be valid.

The views expressed in this work are solely those of the author and do not necessarily reflect the views of the publisher, and the publisher hereby disclaims any responsibility for them.

Photo: Front Cover—Amanda Morris May
Photo: Back Cover—Thomas Russell, II

ISBN: 978-0-595-49944-1 (pbk)
ISBN: 978-0-595-61315-1 (ebk)

Printed in the United States of America

all of OUR Work and Our Words are dedicated to the Loving legacies left by our Grandparents Charles and Mother Frances Strother. Grandma we continue on with your mustard seed of faith and love for the children as we work like you Popa. Thanks for always being there in spirit.

to our Mommy; the foundation of our family. the giver of our greatness our Lil' Frances, our Leader, our Love, our World, our Everything.
Bonni and Chika thank you for making the halves, whole. thanks to you two we are better Fathers and better Men. Millsy, i still adore and delight having you as my world. Chika(CE-94) 12.30.99 & 09.02.04 the rest means nothing from avutu to 303.
to our Sisters Karla, Helen and Lisa thank you for all you've given to our lives over the years. You help us know Family and Friendship.
to our Children Tinesha, Thea, Ale, Osinachi, and Charles our son like nephew—Vinny & Haile all we do is for you. All of Our Work and Our Words are to make this world better for each of you. we believe in your greatness!!!
to our entire family world wide, the Strother, Grady, Boyce, Mills, Chukwuocha, Anderson, Ogbuokiri, Young, Smith, Gasby, Taylor, Crawford, Jones, Carter, Street, Murphy, Lipscomb, Rochelle, Hills; Aunt Fran, Aunt Linda, Aunt Laura Ann, Aunt Wanda, Aunt Dot, Aunt Dawn, Aunt Mary Ruth
Bebe Coker, Bernice Gist, Bernadette Winston, Debra Jackson Spence, Bishop Morton, Pastor D, Rev. Ty & CTAC, Rev. George White, Dr. Livingston, Mama Pat, Mama Lena Harris, Queen Mother Miamonia, Sista Nzinga, Sid & Rita Jacobs, Sis Raye and Kim and the entire CCAC family, the Dickerson family and Universal Dance and Drum. Heaven's Gate Ministry (Rev. Tim and Sister Monique and family).
to our 26 and Madison St. neighbors who are now Family: The Ball, Dent, Church, Davis, Saylor, Laster, El, Hoyle, Richardson, Fields, Harden, Gordon, Sis. Amanda Morris May and family thank you for the beautiful pictures of the Twin Poets and all our work and words—for the book, & nnamdi's campaign.

To Judges Chapman, Kuhn, Brown, Toulson, Clark, Toliver thank you good people for all the great decisions you make to help our community/children.

Uncle Larry Uncle Jea, Jack Booker, Norman Oliver, Bro. Jeff Hart, Rashid Mustafa, Coach Muhammad Salaam and Kenneth El-Shabazz, Tyrone Jones, Arthur Boswell, Ed Lucas and Baba Kamau Ngom thank each of your for the guidance and council.

A special recognition to: all the staff at KCC and PSF—that continue the struggle of reshaping young lives. Delores Mcyntire and the students at Ferris School we've worked with over the years. the SMARTS program at Lincoln University (Mr. H. Bailey and Bro. Mike Gardner) and all the Upward Bound Programs we visit each year. Ms. Em and Mejah Books keep up the great work we see your vision and applaud it. Bro. Mukhan & the rest of the men at Graterford State Prison.

to all the POETS we love to listen to and read from State to State and Country to Country; far too many to mention but extra love to our comrades in work and words who continue to tell the stories America tries not to hear: Trapeta B. Mason, Bernard Collins, Sonia Sanchez, Amir Joshua, The Last Poets, Sunni Patterson, Shake, Asali Devine!, Kevin O'Nieil, Malcolm Jamal Warner, Solomon Jones, Walter Mosley, Peter Muhammad, Life, Lamar Hill, Mtalaamu Acey, Dan Vaughn, KRS, Sadat X, Bro. Aki, Lamar, Ozzzie and Kamika, Ursula Rucker, Big Rich Medina,Blue Chip Faraji, Lorene Cary, Complex, W.E.B DuBois, Jill Scott, Euware Osayande, Muhammad Ali, Nikki Giovanni, Richard Wright, Lucille Clifton, Gwendolyn Brooks, Malcolm X, Del Jones, Wise Intelligent, Mumia, Rakim, Keith Roach, Terrance Hustle Man, Stephanie Rhythm Keene, Chuck D, Sterling Brown, Gill Scott, Rhythm, Safari, Kd Morris/Ronnie Way, Sis. Joyce, Ryva, Lord Jamar, Grand Agent, 7L and esoteric, Pharaoh Monche, Anthony YZ Hill, Black Thought/The Roots, LIFE & Black on Black Rhyme, Sterling Brown, Paul Lawrence Dunbar, Dr. James Peterson HipHop-Scholars.org, Queen Sheba, Sean & Dwayne @ Say Word Mondays, Kito, Osay and Stephanie Renee.

and to all the Poets "one must love to read and write poetry to write poetry one will love to read" Twin Poets

Art Sanctuary and the entire North Stars program each wonderful Artist we have been able to work with over the years you're the fuel behind Our Work, and Our Words. thank you ...

To our brothers, our CREW, our Posse: Walt Love, Pretty Tone, Frank Nitty, Greg—g sus, Bah Boo, Shay, Big Don, Ced, Cousin Marv, Darius and Gene Emmitt (Fat), (RIP CLO).
Before we were men leading our families, when we were beatboxing and freestyling on the corner, before we took overseas excursions when were going to the mall snatching LEE patches, before the fight parties when we formed a cipher to spin on our backs—then like now we were and are comrades; truly we are our brothers keepers

to every man, woman and child
Our Work and our Words
has touched and those they have yet to reach
we dedicate
Our Work and Our Words to you.

In sincere service to our children and community
Al & Nnamdi
Twin Poets

# Contents

## PART II    (KOOL A AL & ELKING)

# PART III     (UNCLE AL & BRO. NNAMDI)

# acknowledgement

to all the Prisoners of War in American Penitentiaries and the families they leave behind especially the innocent children.

# *introduction*

since 1990, the Twin Poets have stood the lyrical test of time, captivating audiences in their message, putting in the work behind their words in schools, churches, mosques, synagogues, juvenile detention centers and prisons, while garnering the top respect amongst their peers and legendary—literary elders such as Chinua Achebe, Sonia Sanchez, Last Poets, Amiri Baraka, Haki Madhubuti, Lamont Steptoe and Walter Mosley.

as master social workers and spoken word artist the Twin Poets have received many awards and accolades from slam champions to coaching little league football championships, from Christi Awards for community service through the arts, to Mentors and Citizens of the Year awards; the Twin Poets strive daily to make a difference in the lives of others, especially our children, with their work & words.

despite never gracing the stage of The Oprah Winfrey Show (Al's wish) the
Twin Poets have been blessed for their words to be received around the world throughout America, Europe, Africa, Canada and Brasil (Oi). their work and words are truly international, a worldwide message supported by their local action. the brothers don't just talk it, they walk it, strut it, stomp it and march it daily as front line soldiers for our communities and children. the brothers support students at a primary education school in Imo State, Nigeria; after their first visit back to New Orleans since Katrina—they began a community partnership to support 10 families; the Twin Poets have, since 1994, run a summer camp for inner city youth. the program and the teen stipends it provides are funded through art grants by the Twin Poets and their community partners.

the Twin Poets have been Artist in Residence throughout American educational institutions including: Camden School District (NJ), Doane College (NE), Gettysburg College (PA), Ferris School for Boys (DE), Agnes Irwin school for Girls

& Haverford school for boys (PA) and for the past 5 years at The Art Sanctuary in Philadelphia—founded by Dr. Loraine Cary.

the commitment of the Twin Poets to present topics relevant to our children is second to none. the passion & power of their words is outshined only by the work behind their words. a parent recently sent a note to the Twin Poets thanking them because her son, who spent most of his time playing video games, was so excited after the Twin Poets performed at his school. he decided that he wanted to be a writer. she said her son begged her to take him to the mall not for a new game but writing supplies and since then he's been writing daily. the difference that is the Twin Poets: after a recent school performance, a teacher commented to the Twin Poets that never has she witnessed such beauty; that "it was the best assembly she has attended in her 30 years of teaching". it did not matter that she was a white woman touching 60 years old from rural america; the Twin Poets touch souls not only with their work but also their words. although, the Twin Poets' performances make it look easy, they truly understand the work behind their words.

regardless of the many hats the Twin Poets wear: sons, brothers, fathers, father figures, mentors, friends, uncles, cousins, nephews, directors, poets, activist, orators, poets, spoken word artist, motivational speakers, teachers, community leaders, aspiring politicians (Nnamdi is running for City Council in 2008—visit www.Nnamdi4council.com) and of course Twins these brothers bring their unique talent, chemistry and flow into it and radiate the greatness that is the reward of the hard work; not only of the Twin Poets but also their parents, grandparents, neighbors, mentors and all of their ancestors that now smile upon their good deeds thanking them for continuing their legacy of struggling to uplift the masses with true empowerment.

from the pavement to the page, to the stage and then back to the community the Twin Poets' work and words seek to completely and accurately identify, address and provide solutions to the problems and concerns that affect our children: from their civic home base Kingswood Community Center located in the heart of Riverside Projects in Wilmington, DE to Avutu, Obowo East Nigeria, to Acada in East London, Otatawa province and our new kin folk sleeping on the dirty streets of Copacabana and Nova gusu Rio De Janeiro the Twin Poets have been touched by them all and countless others from the world's worst ghettos and slums to lavish Ivy league prep schools the message of the Twin Poets inspires children (of all races, cultures, socioeconomic classes and backgrounds) and those who love them to strive to share their stories with the world.

just as our children need to hear our words of encouragement, inspiration and support—they need to see, witness and experience the benefits of work being performed on their behalf to show them the way.

the man who goes ahead stumbles so that the man who follows may have his wits about him.—Bondei

Our Work, Our Words is the definite collection of the Twin Poets—it encompasses the essential force of their message. Beginning with: From Lips, To Ears, To Action … on through to Lyrical Libations and A Protest of Two Brothers—these poems and short stories have not only shaped the Twin Poets, but more importantly the world around them.

* authors' note

circa is listed for creation date on poems that were never written for they were only performance poems

# I

*(albert & nalbert)*

# inner city disease

surrounded in a sea of white t's
that cover the outer shells of hollow men
who pretend they have something positive to give my kids
their misguided lessons on what life is
but sooner or later
we are all going to have to do
what God would have us do
so when a child smiles at you it feels like God is smiling at you
it seems odd; i seem out of place in the house of God
so many sinning in the name of religion
jews killing muslims, muslims killing christians
and so many priest are pedophiles
making it hard for a child to smile
too many scars on their hearts
trapped in the darkness
don't know where true forgiveness starts
forget a pen it's the pain that writes poems
hbo def poetry, but its still pain
the whole world knows the Twin Poets name now
but its still pain
little by little things seem to change
i guess nothing can truly remain the same
when you start cashing checks signed by russell simmons name
but there is still pain
cause money can't heal pain
so forget what the Devil say

that just means i can buy more stuff at the dollar store round my way
i pray to the God of my understanding
that last night was the last night
i ever have to stand in a circle of white t's
i want to live my life at ease
free from the inner city disease

infected with the inner city disease
its doubtful i'll see tomorrow
sleeping with my sorrows
i wake up with my mind unraveling
traveling at the speed of thought
i try to run away from my life
but i wasn't fast enough
my past keeps catching up
i keep messing up on life's exams
every question is multiple choice
but man, their so confusing
the Devil's like, 'look boy just choose one'
God says 'be patient son, there ain't no retest today'
too much stress, so i take recess
go to my old elementary school and watch the children play
but their smiles make me feel a certain way
i grieve, can barely breathe as i watch them run
cause my little brother never made it to twenty-one
instead of tasting death
i wish he never left my mother's breast
stress builds in me
and i'm wondering why is the Devil acting so friendly?
He got me being my own worst enemy
they say the journey of a thousand miles begins with the first step
but so often it's my own feet that impedes the path of my progress
i guess, its easy to see why we're victims to the Devil's confusion

the Devil's illusion

He got inner city slaves believing they're being paid

the Devil will sell you anything that you are big or bold enough to ask
for

the price? is your life

but you won't believe that you've been deceived

until you've been diagnosed with the

inner city disease

nnamdi 7/04

# *he said, she said*

he said i throw i love you's at her like passes from mcnabb to owens
being careful to keep my agenda hidden so she doesn't know where
    i'm going
some call it game, but really its just clever lies to disguise
my attempts to get between those thighs
i say it over and over again baby "i'm not like those other guys"
i sit on the phone with her for hours laughing and tripping
pretending i'm listening,
but if she was a CD … you'd see me fast forward and skipping.
i say it over and over again "baby i'm not like those other guys"
i'm your friend sincere
i don't want to just hit it
but once i get it i'm out of here
i'm trying to steal virginities like a thief in the night
i tell you i love you to give you a reason to be with me tonight.
i tell you i'm trying to make you my wife
but i can only see you on certain nights
sometimes i call just to say hello
provide you with a token when you're in need
i play the gentleman's role true in deed
i call you my sunshine on rainy days
i say beautiful things to hide my ugly ways
i fight back a smirk as i tell you
you know you're my only girl for true
i'm thinking ugly thoughts … while calling you my boo
truth is i don't even love myself
so how could i ever love you?

he said, she said

she said, 'you know sharese—his ex-girlfriend, the one he got the baby
    by?'
she said 'believe me, if anybody knows, its me—the boy ain't no good'
but his words sound so good
he said 'she only said that cause she wants to break us up
cause she want them two to get back together'
his words lift me light as a feather
just seeing him smile makes me feel so much better
he writes me poems sweeter than the love songs on the radio
he is constantly there for me always by my side, he has never lied to me
only open honesty, and the best part of it is
he just listens to me, he is everywhere i wish to be
he gives me the attention i've been missing
since my mom and dad got divorced
but like he said he ain't just my boyfriend
he be filling voids in my life, he told his boys i'm his wife
but it seems that the closer we got the closer he wanted to get
who would believe that after i gave him that special part of me
that night i laid in between his sheets
that after that he wouldn't call me back in weeks
i call and call—but my calls go un-responded to
he don't call me his sunshine, his baby, his boo
as a matter of fact, he don't even call me no more
but when i left him that message explaining our nine month
    predicament
i was sure he would call back, but he didn't
then when i confronted him in the street crying
trying to explain our bind
he had the audacity to just laugh at me

turn his back walk away and say
it ain't mine!!!

al & nnamdi 4/05

# lil' shane

lil shane got slain at the crap game
but ain't nothing changed
except that wall where they
spray painted his name
rip lil' shane

when they killed little shane
they killed the God that was within him
so for one more night they extended the Devil's reign

when the news that shane got shot
reached his pop
who was locked up in prison
he began hollering and screaming
begging for someone to listen
finally the guards sent him to see the chaplin
then he broke down, as he explained what happened
he said, they shot my boy shane!
then he cried manly tears
and said that he was to blame
he said that if i wasn't in here
then he would not have been out there
the chaplain put his arm around him
and tried to sound sincere
as he said i will do all i can to help you get out of here
but, until the day of the funeral
when he gets home shane's mother is all alone
and trying to explain
to shane's lil' sister
why she is never going to see her big brother again

lil' shane got slain at the crap game
but ain't nothing changed
except that wall where they
spray painted his name
rip lil' shane

in the hieroglyphics of the hood
a funeral means food
so everybody came
followed by flowers
from various civic groups and social organizations
then reverend such and such
from the church with the long, long name
said lets have a candlelight vigil
all the politicians came for their 5 minutes of fame
one said we need more police on the street
another said
its the gun manufactures that are to blame
even the black mayor came
and he spoke with such grief and emotion
that some people thought he actually
knew lil' shane
he welled up with emotion as he tried to explain
how he used to be shane
he said he used to defy authority
how he ran with a gang
he said we would fight
but there was never a need for gun
then he pretended to gripped in so much pain
as he screams out
i used to be shane
then he paused, for the cameras
amidst the applause

he received pats on his back
as he walked back to his cadillac and drove off
he was a vet, to this game
and the next day the newspaper
had his picture and his name
i guess even so-called thugs feel pain
as lil' shane's boys
pour out liquor
for their fallen soldier
lil' shane

but ain't nothing changed
except that wall
where they spray painted his name
rip lil' shane

after the funeral his cousin comes around
pretending to be all hurt
then he asked his auntie
can i have shane's clothes
and does his cell phone still work?

yesterdays are forever forgotten
in the minds of men with no memory
because tonight
in the very spot where shane lost his life
his boys once again prepare to roll dice
the paint on the wall
isn't even dry yet
as one of his boys says
who got me faded on a side bet?

if there is another fight at tonight's game
another name just might join shane's

lil' shane got slain
at the crap game
but ain't nothing changed

al & nnamdi circa '98

## _hurt people_

it's those hurt people who hurt people
but those hurt people can be healed
before they hurt people or even kill
for with these words brought into the world
we'll change things of that you can be sure
help them open doors, and find cures
so that maybe one day those hurt people won't be hurting people no
    more
who's thoughts you thinking anyway
you weren't trying to be a thug just a few years ago
you was just a little lad, mad you never knew your dad
tried your best in school, but your grades were still bad
so now you say forget school and hang with those want to be thugs
skipping school drinking and doing drugs
you're all high just walking around
with your pants hanging down
with a frown on your face
a blunt in your mouth and a gun in your waist
doing just what the Devil wants you to do
giving your heart to the streets and giving up on school
got you thinking its just so much easier
to roll this blunt or throw a punch
than it is doing homework and book reports
now you in the streets doing crime
arrested and caught ending up in court
but Young Black Male i see you're not a thug
because i know beneath all the liquor and drugs
is a hurting Young Man looking for love
that's why i'm taking an interest and talking to you
because i know the damage hurt people can do

i'm trying to take the guns out our sons' hands
and replace them with goals and plans
just take a look and you'll see
you don't even belong with that thugged out team
doing ungodly things
sometimes all it takes is a little common sense
to realize if you keep hanging with 9 broke people you're bound to be
    the 10th
so i need you to do more than just pull your pants up
i want you to ask questions ... so you can understand stuff
change your aim so you don't keep ending up in handcuffs
because it's hurt children ... who grow to be hurt teens
who become hurt people with no motivation or dreams
in a world where at age 16 school bells don't ring
only police sirens sing
responding to the hate the hurt people bring
i think i know when it started, and you became broken hearted
maybe when your parents divorced or when your grand mom passed
    away
because since then you've seen many a sad day
so just know she in Heaven looking down on you
and don't want you living this way
drugs and street life isn't for you
just going to end up in & out of jail or rehab
like your uncles and cousins do

its hurt people who hurt people ... but those hurt people can be
    helped
before they destroy their life or that of someone else
for with these words brought into this world
we'll change things of that you can be sure
we'll find cures and open doors

so maybe one day these
hurt people won't be hurting people no more

al 2/06

# *do*

do everybody really love man-man's new lexus with gold rims
or do they just hate the fact that
they still standing on the corner with old timbs'
for it seems that material things is the God that everyone worships
and liquor stores have replaced some worthless Churches
for that's where my people go
to get healed and filled with that—its going to be alright water
numbing their minds to the rape and slaughter of their sons and
    daughters

do

do everybody really love this thick—chick it's so easy to get with
or do anybody love this thick-chick
who it so easy to have a drink and get nice with—then spend the night
    with

do

what do you do when love becomes hate
what do you do when love
that once looked you in the face
becomes took by hate
where do you then find your sacred place

al circa 99

# *TO KNOW THE JOY OF NO JOY*

i heard that God don't make no mistakes
but it's hard to understand when you at a slain teen's wake
they say Joy cometh in the morning
but what happens when in the morning
for your baby boy you're still mourning

TO KNOW THE JOY OF NO JOY

RIP LONNIE PINKSTON

al

# _educational milestones_

Satan pays tuition, for muslims, jews, and christians
infidels don't know themselves
keep each other and themselves
disobedient to God
the difference our teens are talking about proms & parties
teens in palestine strapping bombs to their bodies
they're giving their life for a cause
our kids dying
just because
lil' raymond's dad was in jail and his mom never encouraged him
to communicate so all he knows how to express is hate
but strip him naked
you won't see hatred
you see a lil' boy under pressure
can't take it
scared he can't make it

education helps you view the world in different ways
parents are drop outs still living like slaves
mother crab fussing at her baby for walking side ways
in school they see him as a violent, disrespectful student
but really that is just the way of his world
he can only display what he is shown
high schools setting kids up for a big let down
cause colleges want AP course not college prep now
so a 4.0 to the average university it worth less than a 3.3
in school teachers show their distaste for me rather naturally
then again the guidance counselors doesn't know me at all
assistant principals are like police officers in the halls
if i dropped out they wouldn't miss me at all

their assignments and comments are just more reasons to quit
i stopped going to school two weeks ago
nobody in my house seems to notice or care
the streets celebrate my decision to complete my education there
pats on the back, congratulations
welcome me to late nights and lazy days
a life lived within limits
a future not worth of mentioning
another life soon to be cut short by the Devil's henchman

nnamdi 3/04

# *this is for the children*

this is for the children who smoke blunts just trying to fit in
for the ones who sleep on couches
because they ain't got no beds to get in
this is for the children who truly don't be caring
for the ones where its apparent
that their parents ain't been doing no parenting
this is for the children who don't care about tomorrow
because today is most important
for the ones who couldn't make their high school basketball team
but can still find reality in their dreams to be the next iverson & jordan
this is for that 17 year old girl wondering around looking for love
and by the end of the night
she is going to settle for somebody's hug
this is for the children whose fathers ain't never been known
who live in places
where education ain't never been stressed in their homes
this is for the 16 year old girl whose school bells don't ring no more
now she spend her days making blunt runs to the store
this is for the children who be in school buildings acting a fool
for the ones who never had their grand mom take them to sunday
    school
the only time they been inside a church was for a funeral
this for my baby niece, whose mom's still living crazy in the streets
(i'm talking about a 1st grader who can tell the difference between
    blunt & garci "nah' Uncle Al they wasn't smoking blunts they was
    smoking garciz")
this for the children who got to sleep with they clothes on
because if they don't when they wake up their stuff might be gone
this is for children whose moms got substance abuse issues
and live in homes where you wear whatever fits you

this is for the children

whose parents spend more time in a week at a bar drinking beer

than they do alone time with their children all year

this for the children pumping gas in the rain for some change

this for the children that be goners

whose moms' is getting high again like deandre's mom on *The Corner*

this is for the children who ain't had a real meal in years

only those made by the koreans served in white containers eaten on
the stairs

this for the children who don't believe God is real

for the ones who have seen their best friends and their dreams get
killed

this for the children who sing line for line with these silly rappers

but in class can't do basic mathematics

this for the children who ride around in stolen cars

then sing songs about being arrested and holding bars

mad cause they still sitting in jail; and moms can't post the bail

this for the children in classrooms being all disrespectful

telling the teacher to go ahead and call my mom

cause they know the phone disconnected

this for the children who keep making bad decisions

and ending up back in prison

this for the children, soon to be teenagers

that'll carry babies on their hips like 7 pound pagers

this for the sad children that was absent on picture day

all because their moms ain't have no money to pay

this for the children that got to live with they grand mom

because they can't remember the last time they seen their dad or mom

this for the children with high uncles, who stealing their stuff and be
gone

and for the lil' nieces he be feeling up on

this for the children whose parents ain't never been to their school

for the ones who ain't got money and to get money is the golden rule

this for the children whose own parents treat them foul
and they find courage and strength in the words of Bro. Nnamdi and
Uncle Al
al 11/05

# *act 1*

he was awakened by the unmistakable sound of a pistol being cocked. in the heat of panic, his eyes sprang alive, with the force of the cold, dead steel of the barrel pressed between them. he said nothing. he knew what it was about. His eyes told the story of the preceding events.

nearly ten years ago to this day it all began; that's when he was arrested for the first time—he was only seven years old. he had accompanied a group of older children, all boys except chermaine. feminine, she was not. she was only 11 yrs old and had been through wars. she bore permanent scars all over her body from her life or death battles with boys. no girl alive was stupid enough to call her out, they all knew better. chermaine had given it to all the boys except moo—who was the oldest in the crew. he was 14 yrs old and she had taken him to the trenches, even with her face a bloody mess she had refused to quit.

it was chermaine that suggested they bring him along ("go get 'lil man'") to enter the cracked window of the mills family home across the highway from their projects. The home of john, jr. (J.J.), the spoiled little boy who got whatever he wanted from his father, the local lawyer and city council member. on the last day of school J.J. had bragged to the other kids about his family going to disney world for their vacation for 2 weeks.

moo, tarik and chermaine boosted lil man onto the awning above the kitchen window from there he scaled to the second floor window. it was a sight to see, in mid day. professional burglars would have found it difficult to pull of this job, due to the secure ground floor and limited access to the upper rooms. yet, these mere children managed the nearly impossible caper. once inside the youth ate all the snacks and drank all the juices/sodas in the home. then they traveled from room to room lifting whatever they desired. the older youth secured money, JJ's bike, two watches, four rings and a gold bangle. chermaine would later give the bangle to her mother explaining how she found it in the park. lil man's reward for his civic duty was JJ's baseball glove and his game card collection.

# *act II*

so easy does the mind of a child forget. the days that followed brought smiles, brought candy, brought chinese food and hoagies from the money obtained from selling the stolen items. it is funny how even a misguided child understands the market cycle of the ghetto—where to buy, where to sell. true to their streets of riverside projects (RSP) they would not get picked up like the many who preceded them for RSP—receiving **stolen property**. even with the captured dealers turned informants the intelligence of the police is far inferior to the common knowledge of an inner city child. in a true already professional manner the cards were traded by lil' man for items he deemed of equal value (some to bey for $2 and a handful of BBs and the rest to booter for half a cheese steak from mrs. libby's and a half eaten freeze cup that had been brought for 25¢ from taquanda's mom at the back door to their kitchen.

the klan rid themselves of all the goods except the bike which became a possession of the community, used by any and everybody. it rested freely anywhere without worry of it being stolen; and JJ's glove which became lil' man's prized possession. one would have thought he had been given the glove by Hank Aaron himself. he was rarely seen without it for the next few weeks.

# *act III*

even the brightest sun, will eventually set: the klan's joy ended when lil man (with the glove on), chermaine and moo all sat terrified in the back of a patrol car. prayerfully watching tarik's aunt pretend to be his mother. explaining how "tarik ain't have nothin' to do wit' it". her act fooled no one and he was carted off with his crew. they were taken back to the scene of the crime, where neighbors identified them as the bandits. JJ exclaimed "it was them, daddy; it was them there is my glove". this was lil' man's first of many brushes with the law. his mother, initially, exhausted herself trying to post lil' man's bail. after his repeated arrest she became numb to the sting of her baby boy—her lil' man, being locked up. "shid, he must wanna be in there, just like his no good daddy. i ain't doing a damn thing to get him out!" after a few drinks, and if she was lucky enough a couple lines, any worries about her son evaporated like water on a sidewalk on a hot day.

by the time he was 11, he had been arrested three more times; at 12 he received his first drug charge; at 14 a stolen car; at 16 just one year ago he was placed in Project Stay Free, the Level III community based juvenile probation program. he was court ordered for house arrest with an electronic monitoring ankle bracelet. his home confinement lasted almost 2 weeks before he violated again by cutting off the device. the warrant issued for his arrest would merely join the others (men, women, institutions, systems and crews) that were after him.

Nnamdi 1/05

# _well trained in the contradictions of myself_

from 1776 to 1492,
well trained in the contradiction of myself
i am that brother who stands before you

trapped in an _Imitation of Life_,
where the worst perceptions of me are plastered on the walls of the
    world

i am the picture that is a thousand words
describing all that is messed up in amerikkka:
i am the definition of insufficient healthcare
the only reason a republican needs to end welfare
for the poverty inside of me is far worse than the projects
i am the bastard child
who will tomorrow abandon his own children
i am the reason so many single moms are sitting home right now
    crying
because the 'joy of their world' is like far from zion

i am the little black boy
the one never adopted
the unwanted stolen son of amerikkka
the one you inoculate with hate
i have been given an infinite prescription of ritalin

the God within me has been assassinated
i have been emancipated into a new millennium of slavery
where the whole nation is a plantation
i have been deleted from 3/5 of the constitution
and in the 2 that remain i am bound in chains

my moans of grief and pain
have become amerikkka's top forty music

a brother's suffering is worth nothing
only when i am messing up am i fit to be on the front page of your
      newspaper
i am the book you judge by the cover
the ignorant brother
the one you interview on the nightly news
who knows more about george jefferson than George Jackson
i have been erased from history and placed in an eternal hell
the destination of your designer malt liquors
where dreams are assassinated in broad day light
it has become illegal for me to smile in public
amerikkka has stolen my soul
and placed it on the back of a credit card in the form of a barcode
you scan it to reveal that i am worth nothing
even standing on my tippy toes
to you i am still kneeling always begging for something
i am the alpha and omega of an unemployment line
blind to your help wanted signs
it seems my upward mobility depends primarily on my athletic ability
the rules of society must not apply to me
because when i stand to demand justice
they say to me N please leave these primacies
but i informed them
i've been here before amerikkka's genesis
from 1776 to 1492

i am that brother
who stands before you???

nnamdi 12/00

# *on the way home from the funeral*

young black males sprinting through life
not knowing it's a marathon
because there was no man in their life to give them
the tools to carry on
all they do is carry baggage from one stage to the next
life is simple but their compounding problems
be making it seem complex
and when it comes to death
its like they're raisin' their hands to be next
snatching the breath right out his mama's chest
bullets broke right thru that hardcore persona
his body fallen coincided with the tears from his mama
as she lays over her son's body screaming
no lawd no
i already know there's going to be something wrong with this funeral

they said joy cometh when morning come
but what happens when the morning come
you're still mourning the death of your son
who aint reach 21
sometimes it seem that black teens got life's order in reverse
because before the guns even burse
her son was already in hearse
before the gun fire even came
the choir already sang
something bout this being a day that the Lord has made
but i'm afraid
judging how that gun was sprayed
and how that little girl's body laid
today be the Devil's day

the Lord gone have to come back for his children
some other way on another day

little terik said he wasn't ready to give up his new labron sneaks
so died with them on his feet and his moms buried him in them the
    next week
and when his boys passed the casket that's all they could see
was the sneaks on his feet
all of them talked about how they was hot
and how they was gone cop a pair next week
and we ain't saying nothing even though we know it's wrong
because ain't no way no moms and grand moms
should be coming to a funeral with t—shirts on
on the way home from the funeral
i said its something wrong with that funeral

and the pastor he got it mastered down to a science
he can stand over black babies dying
looking at black moms crying
lying without even trying
preaching funerals of kids he doesn't even know, aint never seen
just so he can get some green
and i hope he doesn't think he is fooling me
with these pre written fill in the blank eulogies
he said the same thing last week when they buried little malik
then he drifted off into some of his sunday morning sermon and got
    lost then
i swear he was about ready to collect some offering
until he looked down and saw that coffin
then he said to all man-man's boys
now how many of yall' what to change yall' wicked ways
come on up to the front and get saved
and all man-man's boys went up to the casket

and repeated after the pastor
how much they loved the Lord
and how they wasn't going be thugs no more
but i know the devil waiting on them as soon as they step out that door
and they're going to go right back
to doing the same things they were doing before
on the way home from the funeral
i said it's something wrong with this funeral

these church folks, they be killing me acting all nice
talking about sister we understand your situation
thats why we are willing to give you the church and the hall for one
    price
that way you can go right downstairs
and have the repast
then they sit there showing false compassion
acting like they listen as she tries to explain what happened
thats when they send sis. margaret in
cause she is the one who also lost her son
so she is supposed to understand your pain
so y'all share stories
and share tears
and before you've known it
you feel like you've known her for years
y'all just sitting back
reminiscing and laughing
thats when the deacon comes back in
and says sister
when do you think you'll be able to bring the rest of the deposit in?
i'm thinking the date ain't even set yet
but i already know there's going to be something wrong with this
    funeral

i'm starting to think its these fake preachers and these greedy
    undertakers
are the ones giving our sons the guns
because they seem to be the only ones
benefiting from his mother's misery
and i heard that the Devil
will keep His faithful gainfully employed
i already know there's going to be something wrong with this funeral

on the day of the funeral
every kid in the neighborhood missed school
who can think about school work
i'm too busy trying to match an outfit with my R.I.P t-shirt
its not about shown respect
its about showing your face in the place
it was more like a social gathering
if their hearts are carrying grief
they sure know how to mask it
as a little girl walked to the front of the church and said
that's a pretty casket
and she said it in a way
that made you just feel her pain
a pain that made her wanna just lay her body down next to him
so that she could be the body in the next viewing
and as she walked back to her seat
she looked over the crowd
and wondered how many of her friends would come on her day
and what the good reverend would have to say
i'm sitting there thinking something isn't right
when our kids are at a funeral
thinking more about death than they do life
i say to myself
there is something wrong with this funeral

i am ready to go home from this funeral
i am in the back pew about to through up
cause even the no-good baby daddy had a nerve to show up
in an all white suit, 5 button jacket with a french cuff
he placed a single white rose in his son's casket
i guess that was his symbolic gestured
to say i am sorry baby boy
then he had a nerve to drop to his knees and beg for God to save him
it seemed that instantly everybody forgave him
because one by one
the people who actually raised his son came up and gave him love
last but not least, his baby mama gave him a hug
and he held her so tight
you might have thought they were going to get back together that
    night
and the rumors floating through the pews
was that it was cool the way he was there for her
and if you looked in his eyes you could see he still cared for her
if you didn't know him
and you didn't know he wasn't in his son's life
you wouldn't even have noticed
cause he was right there holding her hand
for the remainder of the service
but once the funeral is done
and those funeral bills start to come
he is no where around
he can't be found
and beside her mama she has nobody to rely on
no shoulder to cry on
so i walk right past you
don't even shake your hand
cause to me you're not a man

if you really was that boy's pop
he might not be laying in that box

on the way home from the funeral
i'm thinking something was wrong with that funeral
something wrong with these make pretend parents
these so-called social worker, teachers, preachers
greedy morticians, these muslims, these christians
there is nothing wrong with our kids
its something wrong with the life
they are being forced to live …

ITS SOMETHING WRONG!!!

al & nnamdi circa 06

# *inner city shadows*

kids try to live their life all nice and clean
but the inner city is gritty
the dirt gets all in between their self respect and self esteem
and by the time they 13 they've given up on their hope and dreams
willing to settle for whatever life brings
wasting time chasing shiny things
hard to sleep at night because of the screams
he hasn't seen sixteen, yet he's seen some things
that'll turn preachers into fiends
you can look in his eyes and see that he's scared
because tomorrow is coming and he knows he's not prepared
his future looks blank like the T's that he wears
to him God is like his father cause he has never been there
he's never felt His hand
he lives his life like his cell phone—doesn't have no plan
just wasting money and minutes
running circles for gimmicks
soon as the race starts its finished
he does a crime gets caught and sentenced
labeled a menace, but really just a troubled teen
who has trouble sleeping
because he dreams of a father he's never seen
so he stays up late, chasing a dream trying to make that cream
his fate: a murder scene
another murder
another family having another funeral
another mother passing out having spasms
i swear if you sit quietly in the church

you can hear the devil laughing
nnamdi—the bloody summer/06

# <u>*death seems like somebody i know*</u>

99. 9% of the time the hand that holds the gun
the finger that pulls the trigger
releasing the hammer
which strikes the firing pin
sparking the combustion
that ignites the gunpowder
propelling that lead projectile into my body
is going to be another black hand so

death seems like somebody i know

following the flagrant foul
death is the final buzzer of the basketball game
and like a tie-breaking, game-winning 3 pointer
sometimes the shot is cheered and applauded
around here everybody knows somebody that's been murdered
where i'm from children no longer play games like:
tag, hide & seek and hop scotch
they play "guess who got shot?"
children outline bodies
with their sidewalk chalk
i see him walking around
pockets full of paper
proof that he paid for his own ignorance
i see him everywhere i go
death seems like somebody i know

i say whats up to my man shawn
he is finally back in the world
after being down three years
he informs me that his name is "sharif" now

got a kufi on holding a Holy Koran
reciting scriptures about
"how Allah will visit you when you least expect it"
then he asked "you and your brother still doing y'all poetry?"
i said, "No doubt"
he said, "check this out!"
he said he wrote it one night on the yard
he said, 'to the american media
deceiving N is as effortless as breathing
they got us 'waiting to exhale'
while we just inhale, we just IN HELL!"
i said alright, that's what's up bro
i'm glad to see you used your time wisely
and didn't let the time use you
he said "you know how it is Twin
the devil, is just trying to turn us brothers into statistics-
inshallah, he said i ain't going out like that"!
then he said, "all right Twin, i'll get back"
he said "as salamu alikum" as he stuck out his palm
i replied, "wa alikum salaam", as i grasp his in mine
and it seemed that no sooner
than his fingers were free from my grasp
that he turned back into the
same N he used to be
same N he was
same N he is
instead of holding the Holy Koran
he was now holding that golden trophy of N
a forty-ounce of malt liquor
and attempting to hold a conversation
offering me so called illumination
on a book about the illuminati, i already read

i'm like man, i must've skipped that chapter
after he finished advertising his ignorance
i said there is a funeral shawn
i gotta go
death seems like somebody i know

al & nnamdi circa 1998

# *the death of EMMIT TILL*

*by: robert denson & al*

a> al
r> robert

a> one hot summer day
   Emmit Till was killed for whistling at a white woman they say
r> i guess attraction is blind when it comes to color
a> but his blood runs thick red, as does the pain of his mother
r> no mercy comes to his attention & agony fills him till the end
a> his cries & prayers go unheard as he's savagely beaten by these cruel
   men
r> no one can hear these cries but God as his soul is guided by Him
a> and all Emmit's pain is brought to an end as his journey to Heaven
   begins
r> yet friends and family get scared from how Emmit was beaten
a> his mother leaves the casket open
   so all can see death and how his life was treated
r> the smell of his death goes into our bodies, as there is a new
   beginning
a> his death brings awareness so his life is never ending
robert d. & al 3/04

# _Emmit Till_

they said they weren't trying to kill him
just scare some sense into the boy
so that the lil' chicago boy would learn his place
so they smashed their 45 caliber pistols against his face
but their repeated pistol whips couldn't strip him of his pride
even as they rode to his death
he never submitted to the guns in their hands
laying in the back of the truck
next to barb wire strands and cotton gin fan
he wasn't scared of them
he didn't fear them
just as he had whistled at that white girl
the cool night winds whispered that even
at age 14 he was no less than a man
he spoke the truth
a truth they couldn't bare to hear
so they killed him on the bank of the river
as he stood naked to the world
because he bragged about having been with a white girl
a murder that went unpunished
a mother who never stopped loving her son
she wanted the world to see what was done
an open casket
sadness in the eyes of the world
for justice never received

nnamdi 3/04

# *family traditions*

the world was running fast from me
as i tried to run deep into the wound of the world
yesterday a child
today a father of little girls
yesterday seems so far away from today
relaxation impossible in this nation
basketball players respected more than scholars
love and family neglected for dollars
children are their own parents
neighbors wanna say something
but feel they can't
or are too embarrassed
preachers don't even know what to say
when family traditions last for only a day
barely outlived by make pretend men who pretend
to be weekend fathers

nnamdi 3/04

# *rhythm*

me and this little kid
our heads nod to the same rhythm
but as he gets lost in the meaningless lyrics
in the rhythm i find wisdom
the rhythm of basketballs bouncing off the pavement
wraps me in the rhythm of waves which once carried slave ships
the non stop rhythm of slave auction blocks
the cotton pickin' rhythm
the sun up to sun down rhythm
of never ending days
the rhythm of freedom which guides a runaway slave
the pounding rhythm of his heart
becomes the rhythm of the drum
the rhythm of the sun
rhythm

the rhythm ringing in a school bell
the energetic ever-living rhythm found
in children on the playground
that naive rhythm—thinking life will never end
a second graders rhythm gyrating her hips like little kim
the rhythm of swing sets—at recess
the rhythm of the trigger squeeze
the ricocheting rhythm of a stray bullet
teacher screams
no-God please
its rhythm

the rhythm of a subway train
tracks on a vein, a fixed rhythm
the rhythm to which the handcuffs click

a drug dealer's rhythm
the rhythm—of the revolving door on the prison
the gun shot's rhythm
the frozen free fallen rhythm as the body drops
a 911 rhythm
the rhythm of stolen dreams
the police sirens rhythm
the rhythm of the Devil's dance
the ambulance rhythm
your last breath's rhythm
leaving your body as you die
the rhythm—of your mother's tears as she cries
rhythm

the rhythm of a grandmother
rocking her grandson to sleep
while the mother's careless rhythm
has her runnin' the street
the rhythm—she throws your way to make you smile
a deadbeat father's rhythm running away from of his child
the rhythm—of lies unfolding
lives being shattered and dreams being stolen
rhythm

the unimaginable rhythm—of terror which takes over planes
the unexplained rhythm of war
the ignored rhythm of peace

this society's rhythm is out of synch with life
tonight gambles with the unpredictable rhythm of tomorrow
nnamdi 11/01

# OUR SONS — CARRY GUNS

in an attempt to carry funds
our sons carry guns
an so often their families must then carry them
and burry them

....

now Moms even worse off than before
not only did she have to burry her baby boy
but she owe 5 grand to the funeral man next door

....

an a week after the funeral momma can't get it together at all
ain't feeling better at all
but still must play hide & seek from the funeral man and his calls

....

THE DEEPEST GRIEF KNOWN TO THE STREETS

al circa 99

## *to you its just a song*

(dedicated to all those cornball rappers
that can't see hip hop's potential because they live within limits
living for now on borrowed gimmicks
i laugh at their attempts to make sense
their regurgitated flows make me sick
non sense, non stop—not hip hop)


you can't disguise the truth
the Devil is in the eyes of our youth
half of every saturday spent watching videos
far from reality, they got a firm grip on fantasy
our youth risk their whole life, with no intent to gamble
from birth to when they return to the earth
they never learn the value of their worth
their lives are priceless
yet they get pawned for pennies
hurting on the inside
so they listen to these raps songs for remedies
but their pain is not manufactured on a plastic disk
their hurt gets rewound over and over without pushing a button
more than just their monetary investment
our youth give their souls for a chance to be made whole
to these young boys your songs
help make everything better
to bring everything together
for the moment its instant satisfaction
mesmerized by your flow he let's go
and the pain is gone
but you'll never know cause to you its just a song

he sings along with you as you cry to the world
nobody cares
nobody hears you like he does
little kids don't know no better, they take your lyrics to heart
but the Twin Poets we take your lyrics apart
they got drugs and violence inside their community, inside their home
do they really need it in your song?
to them it solidifies the connection between you and them
but there is really nothing in common, you just rhyming
to him its his life's anthem
he listens to it all day long
but to you its just a song

its really not you
its his father's voice he wants to listen to
but its been so long since he's been here
and your song is always on the air
your the new hottest rapper of the year
and he thinks you're gonna always be here
to help him explain the pain
a product of a broken home
your song broke onto the charts
to him it helps to mend his broken heart
his frustration finds a safe place in your verse
finally a prescription for the pain
a new way to deal with the hurt
he gets lost in the false freedom you deliver
as his head nods to your sound
and you can read it in the menacing frown on his face
he thinks you really understand what he is facing at home
but to you its just a song

in you he's found someone to finally believe in
he's found a father
he turns up the volume
to drown out the memories of mom's hollers
he screams along with you
'its all about money, get cash, get dollar$'
in your words he finds his mission
he begins his quest to find what's missing
taking his problems out of the home
but you ain't worried about that
cause to you its just a song

he suffers the consequences to what you babble on beats
now he has to battle on the streets
to prove to the other kids
he is what you say he is
he finds his voice in yours
as you say: 'pops wasn't there
doing what i gotta do, standing on my own two'
every word you say keeps him hanging on
to him its become a way of life
another mother crying
another young black male behind bars
but to you its just a song

do you think about the message in your music?
do you think about the needy kids your song is gonna reach?
what is your purpose, when you say
'you can have school, i'll keep the streets'
your lines have power
to help mold young minds
they can sparkle more than diamonds

get high without drugs
instead of trying to be pimps
you can show them true love
tell them life is more than just
'sex, violence and trying to get your groove on'
help them to deal with the disappointment
to stand up and move on
then it wouldn't be just a song

nnamdi 8/05

# _just another murder_

too many young african american/hispanic youth,

especially young black males are being senselessly killed

the poverty in which they live has created an environment of
hopelessness violence has become the strange norm, the foul
traditions-

in some instances

are the only traditions being valued, respected and passed down

the community response to our children dying is pitiful

almost as if

we are hearing the daily reports about car bombings in iraq or
afghanistan

we are so detached, so uninvolved in our children's lives

it is almost like they are strangers from iraq

nnamdi 6/06

# T.O. and the babysitter

did you hear what they said?
they said the argument started like this!

baby daddy came to his baby's mom's crib
he said, "i told you, i don't want ya' new man 'round my kids"
she said, "stop trippin'
him and his lil' cousin just droppin' off his lil' sister
she's going to do the babysittin"
he said "you heard what i said"
next thing you know her new man gets the rams
and want to handle it with the hands
disrespecting baby daddy right in front of his kids
told him to "step out outside" he said "it is what it is"
out the window the children peep
to see daddy and new man handle business in the street
louder and louder the argument grows
baby daddy ain't even hear that car door close
lil' cousin came from behind and caught him with a couple blows
new man jumps in now it's a full fledged attack
his baby's moms even came an caught him with a smack
little did they know baby daddy was strapped
pulled out the gun and went 'rat 'tat 'tat'
he shot lil' cousin, baby moms and her new man
3 people dead over a babysitter know what i'm saying
but the headline the very next day
super bowl on sunday and T.O. is going to play

al 2/05

# they tell me that i must write

some people call this poetry
but honestly i'm just giving you
what God gave me
see poets used to be scarce
but nowadays they everywhere
you can find one without even looking
i heard they got an open mic sign up
posted in central booking
but please look in my direction
if you're looking for verbal blessings

this is just an essay of my existence
another page in the chapter
my people call resistance
David Walker and Nat Turner
speak with me frequently
they tell me that i must write
to ignite the embers of possibility
that glow within our children
because every night they're being
doused out by 40ty ounces
so often it seems that that the best swimmers
drown in shallow waters (just 40ty oz)

nnamdi 3/99

# *a new crime rate*

the year has changed, a new year has arrived
nothing has changed except the number on the calendar
same hopeless environment
unfaithful gunshots ring in the new year
a fresh murder counts sits impatiently at 0
for less than a split second
before the countdown reverses
revealing the 1<sup>st</sup> of black bodies
upon which many more will amass

nnamdi aba—abia (God's own) state nigeria 1.8.05

## *nothing to go home to*

ain't nothing worse than a young black trying to make a living selling
    crack
except a young black trying to make a living selling crack
with a mom that's smoking crack
so i got nothing to go home to
because she could always find my drugs
but i could never find her love
and how am i suppose to react when i got a pack missing
now moms wants to act all christian
no longer feigning but swearing to God she ain't seen it
and the streets be bringing heat
cats on my back about dough i owe
so it ain't nothing for me to go home for
except some cursing and riffing
about more of my stuff thats missing
that's why I am staying with my man's family
because his family understands me
like that night
when i stung them cats playing dice
i must of won a couple of hundred
then came home blunted
i woke up the next morning with only a couple of ones in my pocket
you took my money and jetted like a rocket
you got ghost i didn't see my mom for like close to two weeks
then you came walking down the street
with your old man wearing a pair of new sneaks
and when he came back out
me and my man ran up in his mouth
you ain't never mention it because you knew what it was really all
    about

i'm only 17 years old and have had 10 years of bad years
because since i was 7 my moms never seemed to care
i remember that time she came in all high to that school board meeting
you told them i was just stupid like my dad
and that i didn't learn
but you were so high you started nodding off
everybody was looking at you like you were crazy
but you was just nodding off
i was an embarrassed little boy
saying mommy wake up please but you were just nodding off
and when i got arrested you refused to accept my call
if i had a 1000 dimes for the 1000 times you told me i wasn't going to
    be nothing
because my no good dad wasn't nothing
i still wouldn't have nothing
so maybe that's why i stand on this corner
holding up this street pole like i ain't got nothing better to do
i just ain't got nothing to go home to

al 2/03

# II

*(kool A al & elking)*

## *why i write*

i write for the youth
who never laid in the grass and looked up at the clouds
for youth who hide on the inside
when the teacher asks for volunteers to read out loud
i write for youth who ain't never even looked up at the clouds
without expecting to feel rain
i write for lil girls who must double dutch near bloodstains
and don't know their father's name
i write to show the youth
that there are far more important things to think and talk about
than the beef between nas/jay z or when the new jordans coming out
i write cause i want to be more important to my son than his pokemon
    collection
i write to help the youth find their direction
i write to explain the pain or put the happiness in words
i write cause God is 1$^{st}$, Nnam' is 2$^{nd}$, and i'm a close 3$^{rd}$
i write to give a voice to all the beautiful everyday things
like birds flying south and leaves turning colors
that get over looked
i write for all the fiends who said they'd never get hooked
i write for all the nephews that know the pain
of seeing their favorite Uncle go from being one of the Koolest Kats
    on earth
to just a junkie always begging for change
i write for relatives who can't relate to one another

for lil girls who were looking for love and found themselves teen
   mothers
i write for the cycle of poverty that never ends in the pj's
i write for grown men who prey on young girls these days
i write for all the rodney kings they didn't get on tape
for all the lil' girls that have to go to court and prove they've been
   raped
i write for the beautiful artist, singers, poets and scholars
whose talent warrants that of athletes' dollars
i write cause a man with a basketball ain't never been a threat
thats why allen & kobe can cash million dollar checks
i write for everyone
from unemployed college grads to drunk dads and babies mommas
who want a better tomorrow but must still deal with yesterday's drama
i write for all the yesterdays and tomorrows
innocent men are going to spend behind bars
i write for jail cells that are filled before the prisons are even built
i write for all those who see prisons as businesses
and wardens as CEOs
so lets build theses prisons and fill these prisons
and see how many minorities they can hold
i write for parents that don't have good parenting skills
the ones that buy outfits rather than paying bills
i write for all the unaccounted hours
fathers spend away from their children
and all the bill money spent on buying drinks for women
i write for all the family trees that died when grandparents did
i write for the togetherness that was displayed when the grandparents
   lived
i write to tell tales of black boys like Donald Goines and Richard
   Wright did so well
i write cause i was also born on Nov 16<sup>th</sup> like NOC and Chinua
   Achebe

and when you hear poems like *I Wanna*

and read books like *Things Fall Apart* they stay with you forever

i write cause the words are all that i have at times

and not a day goes by when the mission isn't on my mind

i write cause God's thoughts enter my mind in the form of rhyme

and my minds rhymes take you to the confines of grimy urban places

some of which ain't never been seen by white faces

so when i address the fact

that so many black teens have never seen their father's faces

they label me racist

so i write

i write to share my love affair of words with the children

because God is on my tongue and the world is in need of healing

i write cause the children didn't understand

the depth behind the deaths of big and pac

i write cause there is no more room at all on the walls

for RIP man man—&—mouky on my block

i write cause there are times at night

when i can't see any signs of life in the children

i write cause i know underneath all those drugs are some beautiful
   children

children who just want to laugh & grin and enjoy life again

i write for the gunshots i hear that still echo in my soul

that tell me somewhere a black life is being stole

i write to make a tomorrow come to this brother that ain't got no
   future

i write for the fake charges filed when they say your son is the shooter

i write for the better days that go unseen and tomorrows that never
   come

i write for all the mothers that had their children killed by guns
for all the i love you's fathers never say to their sons

al 11/04

# why i write

i speak to the children
the ones you could never reach
the ones that live in the streets
the ones you pass by
and don't even speak
then you have the nerve
to go home and write poems about them
so i ask you
why do you write?
see this ain't a poem
its my life
see my words is my work
and my work is my words
so i don't have time for fancy wordplay
i am not that poet
trying to shock you with metaphors
i am the one trying
to stop young boys from being locked behind metal doors
and for the little girls on my block
that don't know their pops
i tell them that they're beautiful, and that i love them
so that the first time a lil' knucklehead say it
they won't jump in the bed with him
i try to open their eyes to the Devil's illusion
during these periods of confusion
when their parents start to loose them
i am trying to find them
by using creative methods
to get the same parental messages across
before their dreams get lost

some people call me a poet
but really i am just a custodian of this chaos
and 24 hours a day i am on my job
and i am running
its like my life is a marathon
running to spend time with my own kids
and my kids that ain't mine
balancing my time
balancing my water and my wine
i live in between my lines
this ain't a poem, its my life
that's why i write

nnamdi 9/05

## these poets

there are times when both i and my God
thinks it's odd that writing rhymes is only our part time job
but we content with things the way they is
and going to keep our full time gig saying the lives of these kids
for these poets here bring harmony and unity to our communities
we perform miracles daily
like getting man-man to squash his beef with budah and them
and getting shaneeka to go to step practice only after she finishes
   tutoring
you see these poets here help mend broken homes
and have young boys
writing mommy i appreciate everything you do for me poems

al 3/05

# _God must know i'm willing_

God must know i'm willing
to do what must be done to keep harm from the children
because it's with sadness that i've learned to live with my grief
as black youth continue to die in these streets
and i know somewhere a mother's dream disappears
with those gunshots i hear
its those gun shots i hear that still echo in my soul
that tell me somewhere a black life is being stole

**HOW CAN WE STOP THE BLOODSHED**
**HOW CAN WE SAVE THE CHILDREN**
**GOD MUST KNOW I'M WILLING**
**TO JUMP OF HEAVENS HIGHEST BUILDING**
**TO SAVE THESE CHILDREN**

i've finally found out what God put me here for
i'm able to see the children's tears that others ignore
i'm able to feel a mother's pain that'll make her lie to her only child
and say nah' baby mommas broke
for she's seen her dreams disappear in the dope her daughter smokes
and the pain never ends
for i've seen black teens who never seen their fathers
turn around have kids then become their fathers
their children share with me their energy, hopes and smiles
through my concern i turn them into my poetic files
there are times when in a sad silence i must sit
to connect with this poetic gift i'm blessed with
i close my eyes then begin seeing God's thoughts
then they enter my mind in the form of rhyme

then the way i word it is the way i heard it
from God with such conviction and feeling

**HOW CAN WE STOP THE BLOODSHED**
**HOW CAN WE SAVE THE CHILDREN**
**GOD MUST KNOW I'M WILLING**
**TO JUMP FROM HEAVENS HIGHEST BUILDING**
**TO SAVE THESE CHILDREN**

Al 6/02

# *G.O.A.L.S.*
## *(Getting Organized Always Leads Success)*

getting organized always leads to success,
helping the children to be their very best
for the children are the future as we all know,
and if you never give up on your dreams, you'll continue to grow
because Getting Organized Always Leads Success

i encourage you to read & write stories & poetry
to imagine and use your mind
instead of just playing playstations and watching videos all the time
read more than your school books & magazines
go to the library and checkout books that are of interest to you
then read and smile as you learn something new
your GOALS become plans a way to make you dreams come true
the world will tempt you and say just be mediocre, try to get over
settle with making those C's & D's that you can get with ease
but i challenge you to study to receive those A's & B's
and when you're on the computer
i want you to do more than go to my space or you tube web sites
i want you to learn how the software works and practice how to type
take no shortcuts take your time and prepare for that test
because Getting Organized Always Leads Success
and the day will come
when someone will try to get you to drink or use drugs
but i want you to think of your mother's love
just say no and walk away
for that persons not your friend
but someone trying to steal your dreams away
and i know peer pressure to be cool in school is great
but your education is most important

so your little boyfriends & girlfriends can wait
pay attention in class stay focused and give your best
because Getting Organized Always Leads Success
and in you your GOALS grows like a rose
so i suppose you should grab hold and take flight
and when problems arise talk things out for there is no reason to fight

and remember your dreams are only a day away
how many times must the Twin Poets say
that no matter how dark it may seem today
keep the faith and your GOALS will make a way
so believe in yourself and make your dreams come true
and the next millionaire, Dr, preacher, or teacher could indeed be you
because Getting Organized Always Leads Success
so i challenge you to always give your best

GOALS a poem by the Twin Poets
for all the wonderful children
to say that hard work truly makes
dreams come true

al 9/99

# *i'm counting on you*

you see brother i'm counting on you
so please understand
for i can love nothing more than myself
which is why i love you Black Man
and i need you
our people need you for true
to help make these black kids dreams come true

*THAT'S WHY I'M COUNTING ON YOU*

i'm counting on you not to be fooled by the Devil's art
for i've seen too many Black Men and families fall apart
after being tempted by foolish things
be it a beautiful woman, cash money, or diamond rings

*I'M COUNTING ON YOU*

i'm counting on you not to react like they say you do
one who thinks with the wrong head and becomes angry & violent
brother i'm counting on you to put an end to the violence & stop the
   silence
i'm counting on you to end the violence & end the silence
to do whats not being done, to say whats not being said
i'm counting on you to save the lives of these kids
because it seems that each time we close our eyes
the black homicide rate continues to rise
as the Aids rate among our people continues to rise
paving the way for our children to die

i need you right now to stand up Black Man and put an end to the evil
i'm counting on you to help save our people

*I'M COUNTING ON YOU*

just like they're counting on you
to fill the new spaces they're going to build onto there old prisons
and to help them pass a new House Bill against our children

brother i'm counting on you
because tomorrows pain gone be felt rather soon
if we don't get these black kids off the corners and into the classrooms

I'M COUNTING ON YOU
TO HELP GIVE THESE CHILDREN A REASON TO LIVE
I'M COUNTING ON YOU
TO HELP SAVE THESE KIDS

al 6/99

# *no time to study*

i have a big test tomorrow i must study for
but i can hear my friends playing right outside my door
ha-ha-ha—laugh kick score
i go to the window and sneak a peak
all my buddy's playing soccer in the street
i have a big test i must study for
but i put the book down and rush out the door
ha-ha-ha—laugh kick score
so much fun playing soccer in the street
i laughed and played until it was time to eat
after dinner to myself i said
i'll study till its time for bed
i read a couple pages maybe 3 or 4
then my dad yells
'the game is on and mike vick just scored!'
i rush downstairs no time to study for tomorrow's big test
just, E-A-G-L-E-S
the eagles loose the game now i'm feeling depressed
upstairs i head to study for my test
i read a page or two as i sit on my bed
then my eyes get heavy and i lay down my head
tell myself i'll just take a quick nap, just get a little rest
next thing i know mom is saying 'hurry up get dressed'
i get to school, break out my book and try to cram for the test
minutes later my teacher says clear your desk
i hardly knew any answers on the test
how did i get in such a mess?
maybe next time i won't play soccer just study for my test
maybe next time i'll watch only a little of the game and study for the
    rest

next time i'll study hard and get some rest
and be prepared for my big test
al 10/05

## teen mother

mothers with little girl's faces

a result of looking for love in all the wrong places

she never knew but now its something she'll never forget

how she mistook love for sex

now she has this baby to provide for, care for, teach and love as it
   grows

but how can she teach something she never did know?

little girl having sex does not make you a lady

your dreams are so much easier to reach without having a baby

so wait ~

al 8/04

# *saturday breakfast club*

aka
'the pancake house'

many would say what's being done here is so un-important
just feeding poor people on saturday morning
they say you're only feeding the hungry for a day
but i say for some this is the only meal they'll have all day
a sacred place
where volunteers help bring those in need out of the cold for a filling
    meal
where many hands make light work while doing God's will
saturday morning at West Presbyterian Church
a place to see volunteers do God's work
you see we do more than hand out peaches and tea for awhile
we help unite families and give hungry children a reason to smile
and for a short period of time, we help ease the pain and clear some
    minds
just brothers & sisters, mothers, fathers & children
seated at tables in God's House
sharing a meal with family isn't that what life is all about
no one talks about their smells or questions their dirty hands
but most important no one is turned away, all are received with open
    hands
we don't look down on them or judge them
for some have just fallen on hard times
everyone does their best to make them feel wanted
like family for a short period of time
week after week, year after year
on the church steps they magically appear, from far and near
no matter if it's hot or cold, no matter if they are young or old
healthy or sick, they all know a place where the hungry can go

a place where they're never looked down upon or turned away
just a meal and a smile to help them on their way
West Presbyterian Church i mean the 'Pancake House'
showing what the true American spirit is all about
no matter if it's the heat of the summer the snow or the rain
a warm meal will be provided with conversation to help ease the pain
not just that of hunger, but the pain of life
where strangers become familiar faces
some so friendly they're on first name basis
just look at their faces when they enter
and look at their faces when they leave
they have a pep in their step as they exit with grace
West Presbyterian Church i mean the 'Pancake House'
showing what helping those in need is all about

al 7/04

# Osinachi — God's Gift

holding my son
makes me feel like God
holding the sun
the power to change night to day
yesterday, he changed me
today i change him
tomorrow he shall change the world …

Nnamdi 10.27.04

# dreams are illegal

i had a dream that i was in america
i was actually in the land of the beautiful
and the home of the brave
my boss came into my office
and said hi bob, how is it going?
why don't you take of early
and here is that raise
as i pulled my suburban
up to my suburban home
i got the mail out of the box
and saw that i was approved for another home equity loan
the girl scouts where there with cookies to sale
of course, i brought a box
as hillary quieted down maraduke who had begun to bark
later me, the wife and kids
all took a bike ride to the park
when we got back we had a snack
apple pie with ice cream on top
then we buckled up and headed on down to blockbuster
to get some videos to watch
when we returned the kids put on their pjs
and we relaxed on the couch in the den
for some family time watching videos
then all these strangers turned to me and said
what are you doing here?
don't you know that dreams are illegal?

gun shots ring in the heat of the night
followed by screams
violently disrupting my dreams

in my neighborhood
i don't have to read the paper or watch the news
to know that something bad happened around here tonight
but once the ambulance leaves, the police sirens stop
and the crowd disperses
that silence soaks into my soul
sobering my senses in this often over intoxicating society
and i try to relax, but the Devil just wont let go
He keeps pointing to the signs
posted all around me that read
Dreams Are Illegal

my neighborhood is the bottom of the barrel
where drugs get mixed
here there are no brothers & sisters
just confused brother & sisters
here people drown in the backwash
of the latest political scandal
in the midst of ghetto chaos
dreams are quickly lost
the Devil is in sweet control
as dreams are stole
and you know
there is no honor amongst thieves
so dreams are stolen with ease
as a high school graduate barely seventeen
gives up her college dreams
for a pair of tight jeans
and a chance to be the next ghetto queen
in the inner city
checks and basketballs bounce with regularity
life and death intermix with no disparity
little kids live for nothing

little kids die for nothing
everyday blue skies are gray
all they know is: they want to make dough$
the Devil has them chasing a colorless rainbow
and at the end there is no pot of gold
just a pot of steam
which He exchanges for their dreams
bonafide slaves are made in the Devil's dream trade
without dreams you are equivalent
to being non existent
our children need to be told that they can achieve
and that God blesses those who hold on to their dreams
we have to take down the signs so the kids won't know
that the Devil is trying to make dreams illegal

DREAMS ARE NOT ILLEGAL

al & nnamdi kwanzaa/97

# _the silence becomes my salvation_

when i was young i was a hyperactive child
my father calmed my butt down
by playing the jazz of Monk and Miles
one day i said, 'dad, this song don't even got no words!'
so he encouraged me to write my own
if i've gathered anything in all of my years
it is that nothing is as it appears
therefore i stand before you naked without labels, titles or names
merely a man without a shadow
in the true span of time
i'm the fifth generation of my family since we stopped share-cropping
but still we've yet to net a profit
so off to work i go
at the end of the work-week i begin a conversation with God
asking Him was life meant to be this hard
the road to success is a dark dead-end alley where i'm from
and all alone i stand
without even a single piece of this world in my hand
i got a roof over my head, pay my bills
but still mentally and spiritually i'm homeless
seeking shelter
i got a concrete backyard without space, place nor time for a garden
so there is no question as to how or why i'll die
cause if a man can't feed himself them how will i survive
my ignorance is shown through my naked body
as i'm constantly stripped by society
then by the overseer's media and even my own people i'm beaten
i begin to wonder how and when will the pain and suffering end
in my mind i create visions of a brighter tomorrow
then my sobs are drowned by the sounds of laughter

that joyful noise of young black boys flipping on ghetto mattresses
defying the laws of gravity
but confined by the laws of society
my tomorrow, my bright tomorrow
becomes the dark day of their stolen unfulfilled dreams
i want to scream
but
the silence has become my salvation
the silence of not wanting to say anything without understanding
the silence of desperate action
the silence of life before death
for the first time in my life silence carried meaning
and it carried me
it carried me back before jim cow
before the invention of a negro
before N become my name
well trained in the contradiction of ourselves
we are dying because of our own fears for living
the Devil stands at the doorway of our hearts
and we love Him
because He gives us absolutely nothing
silently i cry as the Devil begins to laugh
i fight myself to hold back my screams
to avoid giving Him a total victory
in the midst of this struggle
in the midst of this battle
in the midst of this war
which is life i look to God for inspiration
in my soul i find a silent peace
and that silence has become my salvation
nnamdi 11/99

# *this is what i do*

lil' eric walked up on my truck and said, 'mr. mills, i need to holler at
   you'
i said, 'i see you finally trying to get that job and follow through'
he said, 'nah on something serious that's my word'
i told him to 'get in' when i pulled to the curb
he said 'i'm beef'n' with jakeem and them'
i said, 'yeah i heard
your mom called and told me they ran up in her house
what was that mess all about?'
he said, 'i owe jakeem a hundred'
i said, 'the last time i saw y'all was on the corner getting blunted
now he ready to kill you over 100!'
he said, 'that's how it is in these streets know what i'm saying'
i said, 'nah that's the Devil's drug game you're playing'
my mind said tell him you know how the Twins feel about drugs that's
   your mess
go head and step
but my heart said you willing to let this young man die
over a $100 debt he can't pay yet
he ain't say nothing but the look in eyes
said i ain't trying to die
so i turned down jefferson street and who did we see
jakeem and them right where they always be
i said to jakeem, 'let me holler at you'
he said, 'that fool can't tell me nothin' man
unless' he got my money man'
i told him, 'stop being stupid come over here and speak
y'all business ain't everybody business in the street'
he stepped closer i said, 'jakeem why you buggin'?
y'all used to run theses streets like brothers and cousins'

he mean mugged lil' eric and said, 'he know what it's all about'
i said, 'over a $100 dollars you running up in his mother's house
like you ain't used to stay there when your lights was out'
he said this ain't got nothin' to do with that'
i said, 'this has everything to that'
i said, 'about 3 weeks ago y'all was on the same corner getting blunted
i pulled up and said what's that you tried to hide it from me'
one smirked the other chuckled and i knew
God just touched you
i said, 'you look at him and tell him that
$100 mean more than all the things you've done together since y'all
    were kids
all the nights you stayed at each other cribs'
jakeem couldn't say nothing he just put his head down
i reach in my pocket got a bill and gave lil' eric a pound
told him, 'to give him a pound and squash this mess now'
jakeem said, 'that's real mr. mills'
i said, 'what's real is those tears y'all moms would have been shedding'
or that time in prison you would've been getting
i said 'me giving you a hundred dollars
to keep you from shooting him
that is nothing, man listen
i'd rather do it this way
than be giving your mom
$100 for the mortician
not trying to change names
to convince you this is true
truth is this is just what i do

al 6/06

# i'm talkin' to you

i see you now holding up that street pole like so many of y'all do
but i just can't walk by you like so many people do
again it's Twin takin' interest in you
talkin' to you like you my new nephew
now learn life's lessons from the blessing ya' uncle blew
stop tryin' to wear somebody else shoes
and jus' do you
be an individual be proud to be you
make ya' moms proud to say that's my baby right there
when she lookin' at you
son just be you
stop trying to do what everybody else do
use condoms and take sips of the brew
my man i'm talkin' to you!

al 3/05

## *random thoughts ...*

**if i was in this for the cash, i would have opened a
24-hour R.I.P-air brush t-shirt spot called: who shot ya???**

**al circa 2003**

6 o'clock in the morning
i am awaken by a construction crew going to work
i am thinking damn, just what we need another church!

nnamdi circa 1996

**if i would have known that all you had to say was:
whoop there it is, to get a hit
i woulda did it in '86**

**al circa 1997**

Donnie Hathaway said 'everything is everything'
but everything these rappers talk about is nothing
they make rob base seem like he had substance

nnamdi circa 2002

**do everybody really love
man-man's lex with gold rims
or do they just hate the fact
that they still standing on the corner
in their old tims**

**al circa 2001**

in undergraduate i wanted to be an international diplomat
so i studied afrikan languages and history
visited the continent

applied for a job with the UN
but i found it hard to focus on the problems abroad
ignoring those right outside my door

nnamdi circa 95

**so many white t's**
**make it hard to follow the leaders**
**hard to figure out**
**who is and who ain't breathing**

**nnamdi circa 2002**

# the science of love & war

there is a girl in my science class

she makes my heart stop whenever she walks past

believe me she is the reason lip gloss was made

together we could be the Beyonce' and Jay Z of the 5th grade

but there is just one small problem:

and time after time my mind keeps reminding me of this:

**SHE DOESN'T EVEN KNOW YOU EXIST!**

yeah, i know, i'm just trying to take it slow

my mind is constantly giving me

hints and suggestions of things

that i can do in order to make her mine:

**YOU CAN BUY HER CANDY & FLOWERS—GIRLS LOVE
   FLOWERS.**

ok, ok—i say—i get it, i get it.

now one day i'm in science class day dreaming about you know who

when out of the blue, she steps up and ask me for a pen

you would've thought she asked me out for a date

because i couldn't move, i was froze in place

my mind said: **SNAP OUT OF IT**, then he made my lips say: **SURE**

nervously i knocked my pencil box to the floor

then i picked it up and gave her my favorite pen, my sponge bob pen.

she said: oh. i love sponge bob.

my mind said: **SAY ME TOO, SAY ME TOO!**

but i didn't; i just let her walk away.

at the end of the day my mind said:

**GO TALK TO HER, WELL AT LEAST GET YOUR PEN BACK.**

I said see, that's my new strategy

as long as she has that pen she'll always have a part of me

my mind said: **YOU'RE AN IDIOT!**

**He said: YOU GOTTA CHANGE YOUR METHODS**

**YOU GOTTA BE MORE AGGRESSIVE**
**AT THIS RATE SHE'LL NEVER GET THE MESSAGE!**
from that point on beside eating and sleeping
me and my mind spent most of our time
trying to figure out ways to make her mine
my mind said: **LOOK ITS AS SIMPLE AS 1, 2, 3 …**
your right i said, i'll just step up and ask her to go out with me
everyday my mind says: **TODAY IS THE DAY**
but day after day i keep putting it off
and i have to keep reminding my mind
look here buddy i am the boss
then my mind sets up the perfect moment what he calls:
**THE GOLDEN OPPORTUNITY**
everything went according to plan
until the moment of execution
i panicked, and my mind starts screaming
**JUST DO IT, JUST DO IT**
i respond—will you please just shut up stupid!
she turns around and says: are you talking to me?
no i was talking to myself i said
great now she thinks i'm a coo-coo who talks to the voices in his head
thanks a lot, thanks for nothing i said
my mind said: **GET READY CHAMP, HERE SHE COMES**
    **AGAIN**
i open my mouth but no words come out
my mind says: **COME ON CHAMP, YOU CAN DO IT. YOU**
    **CAN DO IT!**
i have butterflies inside, and my legs have turned to fluid
my mind sighs and says: **YOU BLEW IT!**
i am tired of fighting this war
so now i am in love with someone else
because i realized my mind didn't want the girl for me

he wanted her for **himself**
nnamdi 5/2005

# the artist formally known as: $$$
## (for my daughter Thea)

when it comes to my daughter
my heart beats a strange rhythm when i hear her say
dad … dadd … Daddd … Dad Can I Have?
sometimes in a frantic rush
she goes beyond rhyme or reason with ease
and belts out the blues
please, Please, PLEASE
she sings her solo
with one hand outstretched
five fingers wanting to hold cash
but for now hold five point harmony
notes both high and low
father still says NO!
reminiscent of a hip hop dj
she transforms her cadence to the given situation
she greets her temporary defeat
with a song so sweet
she switches her pitch
and goes whole heartedly into her chorus
inviting me into a duet as she explains
dad there really is no cost to you cause
if you pay for it now; i promise i will pay you back
but she never says exactly when that transaction will occur
like i should just believe her
but much to her dismay
i must ask questions that a father must ask
does that mean i should add this fifty dollars to the last fifty or
    subtract?
because i don't ever remember getting that back

but history has never been her favorite subject
so she will never remember that
all of a sudden
daughter smiles
and
father gives in again …

nnamdi 5/05

## words are dreams

70s baby
begun to spit this gift in the 80s
i fell in love with it from the start
when i found i had art in my heart
memorized most of Lanston by my teen years
found my flow during the microphone fiend years
b-boys mesmerized by lyrics since we were youth
that's how my brother & i
ended up with Kool G Rap's gold tooth

blessed with a gift i return from Heaven
repeat what i overheard
for my words are my dreams and my dreams are my words

it seems for 20 years my words been my dreams
revealing things only God & the Devil have seen
putting pen to page
then voicing dreams through words on stage
for when God is on your tongue the young can bring Elders to tears
truly knew my words held powers for years
since reading scriptures in my Grandma dying ears
so don't get it twisted
mistaking the real for the phony
i was a def poet before Russell's people ever phoned me
its not like that spot light was a dream come true
just help more cream come through
its these words that make dreams come true
like having the Last Poets
who your Uncle had you listening to and admiring as a kid
nowadays being able to stop by their cribs and getting to know their
    kids

cipher with them share our works that are new

break bread with them and drink a brew

amazing how these words made dreams come true

and formed a friendship we trust

and i'll never forget when they changed the order of the show at
    bowling green

and opened up for us

its these words that make dreams come true

cause if the truth be told only God knows how far i've fallen

turned my back on Him stepped out of Heaven

i can still hear the angels calling


blessed with a gift i return from Heaven

repeat what i overheard

for my words are my dreams and my dreams are my words


al 7/04

## _compliments_

alex you look very nice today
paul you made a huge improvement
jane your homework is always so neat
hilary you look splendid in your summer dress
bob jr. got another A in math
alice your tan is coming along beautifully
jennifer and peter
i think you both will make fine doctors
gabriel your handwriting
is far ahead of the rest of the class
hank what a neat looking lunchbox you have
marsha your locker is definitely the neatest
billy your haircut looks very nice
tom you have such good manners.

why is it that the only compliments
i ever got were in gym class?

DAMN THAT LITTLE BLACK BOY IS FAST!

nnamdi 3/96

# *essay of my existence*

so many people who call themselves poets are more concerned with
   writing poems
but i am more concerned with making a difference
for me these aren't poems but rather essays of my existence

just thoughts on life that God has blessed me with
so our souls could connect a bit
on the tablets of my heart i scribble page after page it seems
of pain filled lines about the land of lost dreams
home of pregnant teens and dope fiends
where i reside in the midst somewhere between feast and famine
in a land where my people constantly take things for granted
where Satan resides undisguised and pretends
to turn cowards into men
by provoking evil (shoot that N)
and stroking N's egos (you the man)
by provoking evil and stroking N's egos
now the interior souls of my people are evil
for the first time we as a people are facing
the possibility of Our Children becoming a Godless generation
because black youth don't care about God
and the sad part is black youth don't fear God
and it's a

**FEARFUL THING TO FALL INTO THE HANDS OF AN
   ANGRY GOD**

As the sins of the father
continue to visit the Children it shall only get worse
the 3$^{rd}$. & 4$^{th}$. Generations shall be cursed
for i've seen the beauty of the morning sunlight
become good for only revealing the ugliness of last night's gun fight
where bloodstains still remain from where lil' shane got slain

and society ain't say a thing about it
would rather you just forget about it
but for me being a poet is more than just rhyming words
and standing in front of a mic trying to be heard
to be a poet is to open minds and say what ain't being said
to make a difference
to me this ain't a poem but rather
an essay of my existence

so many poets
are content with just writing poems
but this is not a poem
its an essay of my existence
showing not only my commitment to lyrical content
but also
my responsibility as an artist to tomorrow
when i write i try to unite the seen with the unseen
the heard with the unheard
the old with the young
the living with our ancestors
when i write i become the reality of my father's dreams
so many poets are content with just writing poems
poems so that they can enter a poetry slam
and try to get a ten
unconcerned as a 10 year old boy picks up a gun for the first time
thoroughly convinced in his mind
that he's been messed with for the last time
on the subway on the way to the venue
he sat right across from you
hiding behind a mask of emotion he frowned up his face
seemingly to sneer at the world
and you didn't even say
'little brother what you lookin' all mad for?'

you didn't ask him how old he was
what school he went to
or who his favorite rapper was
thats all you had to say
to help this young brother begin to see beyond today
those 10 seconds of questions could have turned into
that 5 minutes of genuine concern that he yearned
but you being the poet that you are
you never made that connection
you never really looked in his direction
or you would've seen that he was seeking your direction
he could no longer fight back reality with his dreams
but you couldn't hear his silent screams for help
but he wanted to consult you his elder to save him from himself
he watched you as you opened your poetry book
and closed your eyes, mumbling under your breath
rehearsing your poetry
a wasted opportunity
because you never realized that your poetry
could've been the tool used to uncover the gold
in this young brother's soul
you could've been that big brother
more than a mentor
that night you could've saved a life
you could've been the one
to reach him before he reached for that gun
but as you reached your stop and got off the train
he reached the conclusion that suicide is the only way to stop his pain
you received a warm welcome as you entered the spotlight
he had just reached the hopelessness of home
as you reached out to adjust the mic
the moments of silence before your first utterance of words

seems like a lifetime, his lifetime
as his thoughts race for tomorrow
trying to leave today and yesterday far behind
while you're on stage struggling to remember your lines
all he can do is remember all the times
his mom said i hate you
all the times he was labeled adhd, and called slow
all the frustrated teachers who didn't have the patience
all the times he was sent to the nurse for medication
sedating him with adderal and ritalin
messing him up so bad he begins to believe it's for his own safety
all he can do is remember all the times
all the times his dad had promised him
this or that whenever he came back around
setting him up for yet another let down
as you pause with one of your dramatic
over-exaggerated hand gestures
he grabs the gun in his hand
his heartbeat can be heard above the crowd's applause
and as you step off stage
the gun goes off

so many poets are content with just merely writing poems!

al & nnamdi 3/00

# mr. brown

the white community protested
don't want those black kids
to go to school where i live
to them it's a simple decision like Dred Scott
that's why my daughter has to ride a bus 5 miles to school
when she could just walk 4 blocks
a father's fight for the right of his child to smile
when she's learned something
earned something
that was rightfully hers
ain't my daughter an american?
maybe not in this unconstitutional southern culture
where the schools are unequal and can't be made equal
her grades are good enough for her to attend
but she is deprived solely because of the color of her skin
freedom, justice and equality
have an expensive price tag
Plessey vs. Ferguson could never pay for the wrongs
done to black people
its easy to define separate,
but not as easy to define equal
my daughter deserves an equal education
just like your children
our children deserve to be taught
and if the local government doesn't provide justice
well then
i will go to the supreme court

nnamdi 3/03

# _this is for the children_

this is for the children who learn math, science, how to spell and read
the ones who set GOALS—for they know tomorrow they'll lead
this is for the children
who love learning & being challenged for its written all over their
    smiling faces
knowing the education they get today, tomorrow will take them places
this is for the children, who give their all and try their best,
on everything from a pop quiz to the SAT test
this is for the children who spend more time reading books
than playing PSPs and watching DVDs
for it'll mean so much more for your future just wait you'll see
this is for the children who make dreams come true
this is for the children who will do all the wonderful things
their parents and teachers knew they would do

THIS IS FOR THE CHILDREN

al 7/06

# *lazy americans*

the night falls like leaves
cool breeze blows through the night
all are quiet
no one wishes to disturb the darkness
we sit with our family and guest
reflect on yesterday, today and the next
ka chi bo, good night to all
at the first sight of light
my people run with the sun
searching for ways to praise God

in america we are made to be lazy
we live a life of leisure
we have machines to do everything
wash our clothes, cut our grass, cook our food
even count our money
we are unaccustomed to labor
i become exhausted merely watching my igbo brethren work

nnamdi—avutu obowo—imo state nigeria 1.1.05

# *a sacrificed cow*

the cow's last sorrowful moan
followed by the rhythmic hacking by men with machetes
in what seemed to be minutes
the cow was reduced to a pile of meatless bones
vouchers flock the sky and the ground
some flying high above
other flying off at the mouth
about the choice portion they deserve

nnamdi—avutu, obowo—imo state nigeria 6/05

## *a reason to smoke*

if you smoke you might as well
just raise your hand and say please
give me emphysema, give me heart disease

nicotine reeks havoc on the internal system of a teen
it takes control, it takes your dreams

and believe me the excuses are all useless

i've heard them all
smoking helps me to relax
imagine that
whats relaxing about hoofing cough?

some girls watching their shape
think that smoking is going to help them keep off the weight
big mistake, trust me
a skinny girl with a wrinkled face
will not get a prom date

and some fools still think smoking makes them look cool
standing there with a cigarette behind his ear
thinking he's a player
but he can't even climb a flight of stairs
can't even pass gym class
and on top of it all he's broke
from spending all his money on smokes

and its easy to see why all the girls want you
i mean your breath
is just soo fresh

let me be frank
you don't smell very well

cigarettes are a stinky, nasty drug
you don't smell it but everybody else does
its in your clothes, its in your hair
i'm going to tell you what all your friend think
you stink!

so besides the bad health, poor wealth
bad smell, bad breath and bad skin
what are the reason you are smoking again?
the simplest way i can say it is:
smoking is stupid
just don't do it …

nnamdi 3/03

# *the life guard*

i'm the life guard and even when there are no pools or ponds around,
these Black Teens just seem to keep going down
not even the best can find their way to shore
many more sure to die in this inner city water war
but i'm just the life guard i sit at the water's edge
then when problems arise i jump in and try to save these kids
but sometimes they are too far gone
and by the time i reach them the little hopeful life that lived within is
    gone

i'm just the life guard

i can't save every one on the beach, i mean in the streets
i just can't get my boots off fast enough
nor swim fast enough
it seems the Devil of death just keeps swimming past us much faster
and by the time i reach them another one passed away

but i'm just the life guard

i'm trying to save these children today
right around the way they're drowning in the bay

i tried to tell them
don't swim in the Devil's water
i'm just the life guard i can't save everybody at the shore
but God knows i'm tired of seeing these kids dying right next door
man—man, mookie, kareem, and shareef
i'm tired of them dying leaving their dreams in the street
one Black Mother in the funeral home
preparing her son for Heaven/Hell

one Black Mother in the courtroom
preparing to post bail to free her son from the cell

i'm just the life guard
i don't want no one dying on my patrol
trying to save these sinking souls

al 8/28/05 jamaica

## the difference between BET then and BET now

a new malt liquor being advertised on BET
makes claims that it keeps N peaceful
N drain themselves complaining about the whiteman
but in reality the whiteman is the
sun, the moon, and the stars of a N's world
and a brotha himself is nothing but a shadow
in an instant he is gone and forever forgotten
overwhelmed by his hopelessness
with a history seemingly not worthy of being repeated
for fear that you may regret your own words
when you're unable to account for your own sins

nnamdi circa 97

# _a few words of thanks_

on the front line sometimes it's hard to find God
hard to find the time to give Him the glory for being alive

when was the last time you talked with God, walked with God?

just being thankful for the blessings

thankful for the problems because they could be worse
thank you for handling my stress
thank you for the faith you have shown in me, for my gifts, my
    ambitions
thank you for using me
to bring forth the changes He'd like to see in the world
thank you for allowing me to work with you, for you, on your behalf
for making me an instrument of change
for having a purpose for me, for my life
thank you for life, for physical health, mental heath and stamina
for my ability to breath, think, read, write and communicate
thank you for the ability to express my vision for being able to see
and read your goodness in others to detect the deception
hear all you desire for me to acknowledge (through my one good ear)
thank you Father, i now understand why you made me half deaf
so i don't have to listen to half the non sense that people have to say
thank you for all that i have, all that you have given me
thank you for giving me a mission/vision in my life
for surrounding me with people who can support, inspire,
and encourage me to follow/forge my life's plan
thank you for my lineage, my history and the future you have planned
    for me
thank you for family that loves & supports me

thank you for protecting me constantly
for allowing me to never experience a moment of loneliness

nnamdi 7/06

## _**mom mom**_
### _(for Ms. M. Deputy)_

my grandbabies call me mom mom
i guess because i was a mom once
and now i am a mom again
i raised my kids
now i am raising my children's children
i don't know what to do with him
he wanna keep getting in trouble in school
well they can do what they wanna do to him
cause this the last time i'm going to be running
back and forth to this school
back and forth to court
i know these babies need to be taught
and they either going to learn from me or the streets
i try my best to stay on them
but my soul weak
i'm tired, i need some rest
but can't find no peaceful sleep
cause when i finally lay down
i still gotta worry about them
sneaking out the house
half the time
i don't know where those kids is
these old bones
can't keep up with those nimble bodies
i been stopped trying
i been stopped crying
all i can do is pray for them
and tell them to do right with their life
nnamdi 4/06

# III

*(uncle al & bro. nnamdi)*

# *God never said*

SOMETHINGS AINT MEANT FOR FORGETTING

God never said we would have sunshine without any rain
or that our lives would be free from pain

God never said all of our tomorrows
would be free from sorrow
God never said
we would live our lives free from the sadness and madness this world
     has
or that we'd only know days of joy, with no days to be sad
God never said we wouldn't have to say good-bye to DAD

God never said we'd have peace and happiness all day long
He never said He'd give us rights without any wrongs

God never said you must be perfect and can't make any mistakes
God never said you wouldn't have to attend a love one's wake

God never said DAD was put here to stay
nor that any trouble wouldn't pass his way

God never said you'd get another chance to say
what you should of said yesterday

God never said that death is the end
those are the words of men

God said in the beginning was the word and let there be light
God knew when DAD was ready to go, he was ready to go
and he was ready to go when he came to get him that night

God never said we would understand his reasoning nor all the things
     He'll do
God said the distance between heaven and earth can't equal the
     difference between the thoughts of i and you

God said he calls the old because they're wise
and the young because they're strong
so when he called DAD, am i to say He's wrong

God said he calls the old because they're wise
and the young because they're strong
so when he called DAD home am i to say He's wrong

for DAD will never disappear for he's right here
in the midst of us now living through each of us

don't let the world say how you have to remember DAD
cause i'm going to remember DAD my way

SOMETHING'S JUST AINT MEANT FOR FORGETTING

remember how just the sound of DADS voice could make you happy
i'll remember the messages you would leave us
"Al & Bonni you better call me its your Daddy"
i'll remember the smile you always gave
as i shook your hand and greased your palm with 20s
because everyone knows DAD loves him some money $
because he ain't even want your birthday cards if wasn't no money in it
remember when he retired
and we got him that recliner
and it was weeks before he wanted anyone sitting in it

i'm going to remember sitting at the table with you playing cards
some how all my quarters always ended up in your jar
i'll remember you & Daryl play fussing
as you won just about every hand we played
and that smirk on your face when you had the high spade

SOMETHINGS JUST AINT MEANT FOR FORGETTING

to the family Mom & the children
we all know that a good man has left the building
its no wonder he was loved so much
just look at all the lives he's touched
all the wonderful memories he left
remember him in health & happiness
not on his sick bed at the time of his death
this is a HOMEGOING service here
for TEE lived his life with cheer
and in HEAVEN ain't no more tears
DAD he's in HEAVEN at peace, and in peace ain't no pain
he ain't having no hard time breathing and ain't hooked to no
    machines
so don't remember DAD in no casket, hospital or nursing home
remember how happy he was when he moved back home & found
    him a home

SOME THINGS JUST AINT MEANT FOR FORGETTING

Bonni remember the smile & hugs he gave when we got him that
    $300 car
out of the neighbor's yard
the next day he was out there waxing it, keeping it shinning and clean
you would of thought we brought him a limousine
but that was DAD, a man who was happy with what he had

because in five years you've taught me a thing or two about family and
   L-O-V-E
Because Lord knows you loved you some REE
Mom he ain't want to be without you
why else he gone be yelling
REE get on up out that bed & make me some breakfast
and later in the evening REE come on in her to bed so we can get some
   rest
and you was right there with him
and when he got sick, you was right there with him
and now he in HEAVEN, Trumella and James is right there with him
Mom he ain't want to be without you
and i know he in HEAVEN still thinking bout you
Ken Earl, Bonni, Wesa, & Tressa it going to be alright
just love your life and kids the way this man did
and to his Grandkids now its up to you to make DAD'S dreams come
   true
so stay in school, watch the things you say and do
for DAD is in HEAVEN looking down on you
remember all the times DAD said
"when i getcha i'ma getcha for old and new"

SOMETHINGS JUST AINT MEANT FOR FORGETTING

remember how much DAD liked to have the family over cooking out
and when he was tired of you he'd put you out
remember Dad and all the times he said
'i'll cut ya' and how quick he could get his knife out
remember his t-shirts with no sleeves
and the towel he carried when he was sweating
Bonni remember how hot it was at the wedding

and how much he was sweating

remember dancing with him at the reception

YOU SEE SOMETHINGS JUST AINT MEANT FOR
    FORGETTING

despite how impossible at times it seems

DAD will live on forever through your memories, smiles and dreams

in the days to come when you get sad or maybe even a little mad

and you just want back what you had

and every little thing starts to remind you of DAD

i want you to look inside for that's where you'll find DAD in your
    heart

for that's where all love starts

so you and DAD will never really be apart

continue to pray and you can still talk to DAD not to his body but to
    his spirit

for through God all things are possible, so i'm sure he'll hear it

DAD i know you at peace not in no pain

descending from Heaven the chariots came to take you from this
    world of flames

DAD the Heavenly angels are calling your name

DAD even the winds are whispering some how

and i know you're in Gods hands now

so to the family no matter what those of this world may say

we know for DAD it's a new day and in heavenly happiness he'll
    forever stay

now he's free from the restraints of this world of old

for we know his heart was pure, so his streets are now gold

yes, DAD you'll be missed
but go on to Heaven and get your rest

your family loves you DAD but he Creator
loves you greater

rest in peace for God knows best
sleep on DAD forever get your rest
rest in peace for God Knows best
sleep on DAD forever get your rest
SOMETHINGS JUST AINT MEANT FOR FORGETTING
REST IN PEACE DEMPSEY "TEE" TAYLOR
LOVE "YOUR FAVORITE SON-IN LAW"

BECAUSE SOMETHINGS JUST AINT MEANT FOR
    FORGETTING

al 1/04

# i wish i could go back (for Unc. Ant)

flipping through the pages of a photo album
i am reminded of what life is about and sometimes i wish i could go
    back

i wish i could go back to this picture of my favorite x-mas
i remember i was on honor roll so mom got me everything on my list
a couple of kangols, green suede pumas
a rope chain with a medallion that read my name
a swatch watch, a boom box and two tapes
T La Rock and Dougie Fresh instrumental beatbox
i was in b-boy heaven
i thought i was dreaming as i spun on my back

sometimes, i wish i could go back

i remember waking up just two days after x-mas to find all my new
    stuff missing i'm thinking maybe my mom put it somewhere
so i looked all over the house even down in the kitchen
i checked every room, every closet—but its still missing

in the basement i find my uncle sitting with his eyes glistening
i asked him "have you seen my stuff?"
but he just nodding
he not even listening
and when i looked in his eyes it hurt
cause i realized i had become the latest victim to my uncle's addiction

my mom replaced all the stuff
but there is something missing in me she can never give back

sometime i wish i could go back

i wish i could go back to when the pain was gone
as i look at this picture of my uncle in his high school football uniform
i remember telling everybody i wanted to be just like you
when all the other kids wanted to be like Dr. J or Kareem Abdul-
    Jabbar
when OJ Simpson was running through airports
and Reggie Jackson had his own candy bar
you were my uncle and you were my hero
you were the pride and joy of our family
you were the all-state, college bound running back
i remember my brother and I would stay up late
to hear your often over exaggerated after game recaps
you'd tell us how the other team had an illegal defense
with 12 men on the field and they still couldn't stop you
cause you were just 'the man'
how you scored three touchdowns with three men on your back
sometimes, i wish i could go back

i wish i could go back to this picture
where you were all dressed up in your tux for your high school prom
i wish there was something, anything i could do
to prevent that girl that is with you from becoming your son's mom
although i love my little cousin
i just wish he had came at a later time
then maybe you would have had the opportunity
to go to michigan state instead of graduating to the university of
    vietnam
you said you had to take care of your son
so instead of running with the ball you were now running with a gun
if you never went to vietnam
you probably would have never been introduced to drugs

and you wouldn't have been a junkie when you came back
so, honestly i just want my Uncle Anthony back!

nnamdi 5/03

# *Mother Rochelle*

one only needs to look into your eyes to see how important family is
you've been there for your kids & for your kid's—kids
only God can count all the helpful things you did
you're the answer to so many prayers
you've made so many dreams come true
Mother Rochelle there's not another on earth like you

there's nothing on earth like the love of a Black Mother
not that of a father, sister nor brother

its Grandmom's love that keeps this family together
and it's your desire that the family not only get bigger, but better
and still stick together, forever
you've felt God's hands a few times so you know He exist
so it's to no surprise you've been blessed with a gift
like how you can look them in the eyes
and separate the truth from the lies
and how you always made a way right on time when it was needed
and how you never turned your back on your kids not even when it
    was needed
you made sure your kids knew love
and looked out for one another
from sister to brother love came down from the Mother

for there's nothing in the world like the strength of a Black Mother,
not that of a father, sister nor brother

for a Black Mother's pride is the whole family's guide
through good, through bad she's at your side

for even when everyone else gives up on that family member gone
   wrong
it's a Mother's love that still stands strong

amazing is your grace
i can see God in your face
continue to live well, laugh often, and love much
for nothing can match a Grandmother's touch
you love your family like Christ loves the church
that's why you always put your babies first
there's no limit to what Mother Rochelle will do
for her Gayle, Frank, Linda, Reno, Penny, and Boo
you showed the way through love the advice of a lifetime
a special Mother, one of a kind

al 7/05

## *it shouldn't take a funeral to make a black family hug*

in search of peace and success in this land of confusion
but in the process Black Family love we are losing
living in the same town
but it takes bad news to bring you around
when we were young Grand mom kept the family tight
family was always over
then we'd ask if our favorite cousins marvin, darius or gene could
    spend the night
big sunday dinners with all the family over
but now it seems like those days are over
and then we make a promise every time before leaving
that it won't be so long before out next meeting
and that it definitely won't be a funeral
but deep in the back of our minds the truth we all know
for today's Black Families are not as close as we should be at all
because we barely visit or have time to call
but we're at your bedside quick
when we get the word you're sick
in the past it was nothing to pack up the car and drive to Georgia or
    Carolina
but today's Black Families just can't find the time
Black Families came together not only in sickness but in good health
not just to cry broke but also to share the wealth
they came together not only at funerals and weddings
but each time a child was born
truthfully i don't know where those days have gone
because i have cousins younger than i,
that i wouldn't know if i passed them by
are we missing the Strong Black Woman

or has the Black Man just gotten weaker
this question is puzzling i can't answer it either
what's wrong with the Black Family my shoulders i have to shrug
because It Shouldn't Take A Funeral To Make My Black Family Hug

I KNOW ITS THERE SO LETS EXPRESS THIS LOVE
BECAUSE IT SHOULDN'T TAKE A FUNERAL
TO MAKE MY BLACK FAMILY HUG

in search of peace and success in this land of confusion
but in the process Black Family love we're losing
it's nothing like the past when togetherness and love were overflowing
for today it's just not showing
sometimes it just doesn't seem fair
i almost want to call Be Be and Ce Ce and ask them to "Take Me
    There"
to a time when the Black Family was tighter
and the black man was a lover not a fighter
when one of my uncles was always there to give advice on any topic i
    could think
instead of coming around bumming money for a beer to drink
and when my aunts were strong women and their families they'd lead
instead of crying about the kids she has to feed
and what a hard time she's having meeting their needs
i don't understand how they expect this young boy to become a man
when there are no real role models for him to follow
why are today's Black Families full of empty promises and a lot of
    fronting
why does family only come around when they want something
a perfect example of this is if you hit the lottery they are underneath
    you
but they are nowhere to be found when you're in need of a few
i pray one day we can make it like it was
caring, extended families with lots and lots of love

when Bibles were on the tables and not liquor bottles
and Pops was at home, an in house role model
what's wrong with the Black Family my shoulders i have to shrug
another funeral brings us together, now once again we're showing love
But IT SHOULDN'T TAKE A FUNERAL TO MAKE MY BLACK
    FAMILY HUG

I KNOW ITS THERE SO LETS EXPRESS THIS LOVE
BECAUSE IT SHOULDN'T TAKE A FUNERAL
TO MAKE A BLACK FAMILY HUG

al 6/92

# yesterday when i was in heaven

yesterday when i was in heaven they acted like they didn't want to let me in

so i messed up my hair and came back and pretended i was my twin

yesterday when i was in heaven there was a mad poet emcee cipher going on

brothers were freestyling to Miles blowing his horn

then out of nowhere came dj Scott La Rock

and he was doing the beat box for Big & Pac

when i was in heaven yesterday i was surprised

to see God really was a white man with blonde hair and blue eyes

a big fat guy who used words like golly willicker and narley

and rode around heaven on his harley

yesterday when i was in heaven i got pissed

because God wouldn't put guinness on the drinking list

(yall' aint got no guinness up here?)

and other folks were cooking so i could only get a piece of baked fish

(yall' don't fry no fish up in here?)

when i was in heaven yesterday God took me to a playground

i got to see all the kids who had been murdered or aborted

God said you see that little girl right there with the bows in her hair?

that was going to be your daughter you aborted

when i was in heaven yesterday

yesterday when i was in heaven

i looked God dead in the eyes and i couldn't deny the resemblance

since i was made in His image; me, Him and my twin looked like triplets

yesterday when i was in heaven

i made Wilma Rudolph and Flo Jo smile

as i got walked down by Jessie Owens in the ¼ mile

but i was happy to get second place
as i stood on the podium
like Tommy Smith & John Carlos in 1968

yesterday when i was in heaven
i was invited to a poetry spot called:
the burning bush—Claude McKay and Zora Neal were hosting a
    poetry slam
the winner got to get his or her writings put in the next bible

yesterday when i was in heaven
God granted me a wish
He said, 'close your eyes and whatever you wish for
when you open them it shall appear'
i closed my eyes, and i wished to see what my life would have been like:
if afrikans were never brought to america
when i opened my eyes there i was as a young man growing up in
    nigeria
speaking igbo, living in the state of imo
in a small village called owerri
and i had no worries for it was my grandfather
who with the use of his poetry helped prevent the war in biafra

yesterday when i was in heaven
i sat at the feet of our ancestors
and as we discussed the state of the black nation
i watched them begin to cry libation

yesterday when i was in heaven
i split kola nuts with Nnamdi Azikiwe
i had palm wine with Patrice Lumumba
i had gari, fufu and mai-mai with Sundiatta from mali
and i told him how his life's story would forever be remembered
because disney made it into a movie called the lion king

i told Shaka Zulu that the unity he was striving to bring
is now being forged by both the inkatha and the ANC

yesterday when i was in heaven
my face flooded with tears
and i screamed at God what is Idi Amin doing here?

yesterday when i was in heaven
yesterday i was in heaven ...

al & nnamdi 7/00

## *Osinachi*

my son gets bigger each time i look at him
was he not so small only 4 months ago
that he slept inside his mother's belly?
his legs and arms are strong
but even mightier is his smile

nnamdi avutu, obowo—imo state nigeria Xmas 04

# _Baba Chukwuocha_

he remembers his last word only until it leaves his tongue
who are you?, says my father
Baba, i am Nnamdi, this is Osinachi your grandson
how painful it must be to have others tell you who you are
how joyous it must be to hear them say good things
a life well lived
devoted to his wife, his family and all the village's kids
a true elder, a true teacher
the instructor of chiefs
blessed to touch the soul of a child
making it impossible for anyone
to say Baba without a smile

nnamdi avutu obowo—imo state nigeria 1.1.05

## *no home to go home to*

he said i should be happy i was brought here to america
he said if it wasn't for the christians on their civilizing missions
i'd still be in africa—with those uncivilized savages
the backward people of the world, who have no history nor future
he said i should be grateful, i was brought to this great land
happy to call america, my home
but in my heart i can never call america my home
if it was my home they wouldn't treat me the way they do
and if what he says about africa is true
i don't wanna go back there
so i feel like i'm trapped between these two lands
with no home to go home to
he got me sharecropping on a piece of worthless land
and it seems like the more i make
the more he takes
so no matter how much work i do
i'm still in debt to you
season after season, a bigger balance is due
at the end of the harvest
i ain't got nothing to go home to
when i thought about moving north
he said you can't go nowhere
until you pay me what you owe me
i own you
i ain't got nothing to go home to
my children can't go to school or even play
like other kids do
they gotta help me work in the fields
cause all that i owe you
so in the eyes of my kids

thanks to you
home ain't no home to come home to

they got me working
working to survive, doing odd jobs
praising their god
seems like even the salvation of my soul
is being used to maintain their life of leisure
now my heart could never explain somebody else's pain
but why would she say i raped her
when in reality
she couldn't keep her hands off me
she told me not to tell a soul
then she going to go cross me
now they are burning crosses all around town
burned my house down to the ground
i don't know what to do
cause i don't have no home to go home to

they got their dogs and their guns
they are coming after me, for something i didn't do
in her heart, she knows its true
i refuse to die for her lie, to be blamed for her shame
my wife said, you can try to explain but the truth they ain't gone
    believe
they ain't going to be happy until they see you on one of those trees
my grand mom broke down to her knees
and said, child please leave
she said if you don't leave tonight
you won't live to see the morning light
so now i'm running
i know where i'm running from
but don't know where i'm running to

i feel like i don't got no home to go home to
i'm running
running through the darkness of the woods
i am guided by the light of my mother's smile
i remember being taken out of her arms as a child
i'm running
like i am racing against my childhood memories
i remember my grandmother telling me
that i laid in the blood that spilled when my father got killed
she said that spirit never dies
she said that's why they call me nnamdi
cause it means my father is inside of me
she said that igbo our native tongue
from the land east of benin where our people come from
so although it seems like i don't
i really do have a home to go home to
i wish i could run back to those african shores
but i can't
i run until i can't run anymore
but my mind is still running
thinking about my family and how much they're going to miss me
as i stand on the banks of the mississippi
i say to God, that i don't know what to do
then the face of the river became the face of God
and He smiled
and said come on home child, you have a home to come home to
and it seemed that the more the river roared
the more God said He loves me
then He stretched out His arms
as if He was just waiting to hug me
as my feet leave this loveless land
i hear my grandmother on her knees prayin/sayin

'precious lord please take my baby's hand'
although it's the middle of the winter
the water was warm
this world can't do me no harm
cause now i'm in God's arms
and i know He's real
i can feel Him holding me tight
as i'm carried under and away by the river
i don't fight
cause i know God is going to bring me home tonight

nnamdi 2/03

# _She_

_for my Chika, my sisters Ijeoma and_
_Christiana in Aba_

she has given the world her everything and has received nothing in
    return

her back yard has become the breeding place of corruption

she smiles even when it hurts

even with the weight of poverty placed upon her she holds her head
    high

she taught the world to stand upright and is now forced to bow to
    their power

she sleeps where bare feet meet developing streets

where a bus full way beyond capacity stops to pick up more passengers

she stands before the world in the nude displaying her negritude

she was stripped of her yesterday

and given a glance at someone else's tomorrow

her identity is under siege

with her faith religion became real

she has fanned the winds of war

her village comes together for communion at night

she hits the ground running with the first sight of daylight

she was forced to give up her faith and traditions

she was called primitive

tricked into glorifying a false God that doesn't exist

she bares the pain of an afrikan poet who has never written a poem in
    her own

even after nepa has taken her lights she still shines bright

she spoke to me with love

when she spoke i repeated her greetings

my words tickled my mouth and made us both smile

her subtle tones holding me like a child
i make promises to marry her and stay with her forever
she resides within extreme poverty
where every family has wealth
that the size of the compound could never measure
where there are the conditions to create violence
here schools teach a path of peace
she is a people, a culture all her own
she is the reason men go to war
she is the world's finest
she works hard for far less than she deserves
even in her whispers she has the power to be heard
she has a timeless history
she wakes me up/welcomes me
she is familiar to me in ways unknown to myself
she (is) has a language all her own
she has a faith which has endured many test
she is children smiling and playing
she is men & women who are sincere while praying
she is smiles while dancing
my memory of her was washed clean during the middle passage
her customs and traditions were thought to be primitive
un-useful in the modern world
stripped of her everything and given oppression
raped by the world
yet she still embodies the minds, fruits to feed/power the world
she smiles through her sorrows
she needs no reason to be thankful and to praise God
she dances a dance that moves the world
the places we would hate to visit she calls home
she is a school with no modern books or equipment, yet full of
    learning

she is life in its purest form
under military rule her name was changed to corruption
she is a shinning sun in a gold ashoke
she has the hands which give life to fabric

she is Africa, at its best
she is NIGERIA
nigeria kwenu?
yaa
igbo kwenu?
yaa
Avutu kwenu?
yaa
nnamdi—owerri—imo state—12/99

# Sistah Nzinga

Queen Sistah Mother

cares for her family & people like no other

Gods in her heart first and foremost

we love how you love Black folks

Sistah Nzinga

you didn't just say support Black business

you opened a business and kept it open

better tomorrows for your family is what she's hoping & why she
working

doing right for those who at times don't even do right by you

Sistah Nzinga doing just what God would have you to do

i recall your battles with your babygirl head to head

when Silver had a hard head

almost broke your back—but you ain't never turn your back

through it all she always knew where love & home was at

now look what Sistah Nzinga's love done did to that hard head

all a testament to the way you live and raise your kids

Sistah Nzinga that strong Black Mother that doesn't give up on her
kids

just keep putting the goodness God gave you in their heads

we're proud of you Sistah Nzinga & all you do

for 50 years you walked the walk & talked the talk for us

Twins just wanted to say Happy Birthday

and thank you for all the love & trust

you've always given us

thanks for noticing the gift and helping inspire us to reach goals

when others didn't understand the poetry & prose in our flows

one of the few women we've ever seen

always on the frontline for our people

always been Mother Sistah & Queen

service to her people always sincere
Twin Poets just wanted to let you know
how glad we are that Sistah Nzinga is here
Queen Sistah Mother
sistah our people love you
on both sides of the atlantic
you are a true reflection
of our afrikan connection
you are the truth
refuting the lies we have been told
holding mother afrika always in your soul
you demonstrated quiet defiance
when they said we were not afrikan
and that real afrikans did not care about us
they said we were the lazy children of slaves
your 50 years corrects
the hundreds of years of lies
told to the world
you showed the world
exactly what we could be when we
love and support one another
when we live as sisters and brothers
always got your people's back
solidarity in your stance
God moves within you when you dance
from your bare feet welcome dances on market street
to the marketplace in Avutu, Obowo, Nigeria
nothing speaks clearer than your body language
your movement, your dance, your poem to the world
the reality of Marcus Garvey's dream

always our Sista, Mother, Queen
**Happy 50<sup>th</sup> Birthday Sista Nzinga**

al & nnamdi 11/2007

# _free_

my eyes search the sky
as i'm askin God
please send me a sign
telling me that what i'm about to do
is what He want me to do
cause i'is ready to run away today
just then the thunder sounds
throughout the underground
and i realize God's coming
and i'is running

i'is been runnin for days
runnin for weeks
during the day i hide
high in the treetops
is were i sleep
fruits and berries is all i'is eat
my body is weak, but my soul is strong
and when i think about my freedom
this road don't seem so long

and i'is jus keeps on runnin
and it hurts but i'is jus keeps on runnin
cause i'is got kin that i'is knows i ant never gone sees again
so i'is jus keeps on runnin

not runnin from my wife
but for my wife
to give her and our kids
the life they deserves to live

so i'is jus runnin
runnin from the slave catchers
cause i'is ain't nuthin
but a piece of stolen southern property
under these fugitive slave laws
so i'is running

i'is jus keeps on runnin
runnin from the slave catchers tryin to chase me
into the arms of my ancestors jus waitn to embrace me
i reaches philadelphia and finally i'is be free

nnamdi 4/06

for more information regarding the Twin Poets, please visit www.
TWINPOETS.com

email: TWINPOETS@aol.com

to purchase more books
send orders to: books@TWINPOETS.com
also available:
Selected Poems (96)
Lyrical Libations (98)
Audio
From Lips, To Ears, To Action … (98)
One Nite in New Jerusalem (live 00)
Twin Poets live at Warmdaddies (01)
A Protest of Two Brothers (04)
Video
Twin Poets @ UD (96)
Twin Poets @ Painted Bride
Twin Poets—Kings of Poetry
Twin Poets—Def Poetry (Dreams are Illegal)
Twin Poets—Def Poetry—(Interview with a Wack Emcee)

Twin Poets for Project ACT.

978-0-595-49944-1
0-595-49944-9

CPSIA information can be obtained at www.ICGtesting.com
Printed in the USA
BVOW062217110412

287464BV00001B/4/P